# A BRIEF HISTORY OF SERBIAN MUSIC

By William Dorich

Published by
GM Books—Los Angeles

# Credits

| | |
|---|---|
| Compiled & Produced by | William Dorich |
| Editor | Basil W. R. Jenkins |
| Project Director | Anita Dorich |
| Text by | † Isidor Bajic |
| | Paul S. Bielich |
| | William Dorich |
| | † Stana Djuric-Klajn |
| | † Dr. Stojan Lazarevic |
| | † Ed Levine |
| | Paul S. Papich |
| | † Helen Leah Reed |
| | † Manuel Trbovich |
| Historical Advisors | Dr. Milos Velimirovic, Prof. Emeritus, University of Virginia |
| | † Dr. Alex Dragnich, Prof. Emeritus, Vanderbilt University |
| | Basil W. R. Jenkins (Byzantine Scholar) |
| Book Design | William Dorich |
| Religious Consultants | His Grace Jovan, Bishop, Serbian Orthodox Diocese of Western America |
| | † Archimandrite Dositei Obradovich |
| | Very Rev. Nicholas Ceko, Dean, St. Steven's Serbian Orthodox Cathedral, Alhambra, CA |
| | Rev. Father Blasko Paraklis, Rector, The Nativity of The Holy Theotokos Serbian Orthodox Church, Huntington Beach, CA |
| Production & Printing | GM Books, Los Angeles—Hong Kong |
| ISBN | #9781882383054 |

All Rights Reserved
Third Edition
November, 2011
Printed in the USA

*Cover Illustrations:* Milan Kecman (Reproduction Rights Reserved)

*Title Page*: Depicts a page from the *Mokranjac Liturgy*, published in 1964 by the Belgrade Choral Society. Photo of Stevan Mokranjac (1859-1914), considered the most revered Serbian composer of his time. He is portrayed here wearing numerous medals, including *The Order of St. Sava,* which was bestowed on him by the Holy Synod of Serbian Orthodox Bishops.

Photo courtesy of † Archimandrite Dositei Obradovich.

*This book was inspired by the research of
Professor Stana Djuric-Klajn
and is dedicated to the singers and musicians
in the diaspora who devoted their lives to
preserving Serbian music.*

# Contents

**PREFACE**
*Dr. Milos Velimirovic*.................................................................. 6

**INTRODUCTION**
*William Dorich*........................................................................... 8

**DEATH OF A GUSLAR**
*Isidor Bajic*................................................................................ 9

**SERBIAN COMPOSERS FROM 1826-1932**
*William Dorich*......................................................................... 10

**SERBIA**
*Helen Leah Reed*...................................................................... 31

**MUSIC IN THE FEUDAL ERA**
*Stana Djuric-Klajn*................................................................... 33

**CHURCH MUSIC**
*Stana Djuric-Klajn*................................................................... 36

**HYMNS & SURVIVING MANUSCRIPTS**
*Stana Djuric-Klajn*................................................................... 41

**SERBIAN MUSICAL LIFE IN THE 18TH CENTURY**
*Stana Djuric-Klajn*................................................................... 47

**MUSIC DURING THE REIGN OF PRINCE MILOS**
*Stana Djuric-Klajn*................................................................... 52

**THE BELGRADE CHORAL SOCIETY 1853-1953**
*Dr. Stojan Lazarevic*................................................................ 57

**VLAJKO—THE MAN AND HIS MUSIC**
*Paul S. Bielich & Paul S. Papich*............................................. 66

**SERBIA: SINGING**
*Helen Leah Reed*...................................................................... 75

**VINKA—BORN TO SING!**
*William Dorich*......................................................................... 80

**A LIVING LEGEND—THE POPOVICH BROTHERS**
*Manuel Trbovich & Ed Levine*.................................................. 84

**TAMBURITZA—SERBIAN MUSIC IN 20TH CENTURY AMERICA**
*William Dorich*......................................................................... 91

**PHOTO COLLECTION**
.................................................................................................. 117

**EPILOGUE**
*William Dorich*......................................................................... 129

# Preface

It is, indeed, a pleasure for every American of Serbian origin to discover and examine this volume which presents a solid introduction to the history of Serbian music. Yet even more important is the fact that the compiler and producer of this book, William Dorich, has for the first time (to this writer's knowledge) assembled in one place as large a collection of data about the musical activities of many individuals and of tamburitza orchestras of Serbs that performed folk music and popular music for the Serb settlers in the United States. When to this volume one may add a companion volume—a survey of, and the archival data about the activities of Serbian choral associations and church choirs, one will be able to gain a deeper insight into the contribution of Serbs to the cultivation of the art of music in the US. Furthermore, it will represent a significant contribution toward the history of music of Serbs in general.

The history of Serbia has not always enjoyed conditions favorable for the flourishing of the art of music. The medieval heritage of Serbs contains superb examples of frescoes in monasteries and written documents of the literary activities of Serbs. As far as the musical art is concerned, only scattered references about some musicians exist before the 15th century—and then we do find the names of a handful of chanters as well as composers of hymns for the religious services. Their works are preserved in Byzantine musical notation that escaped the attention of the scholarly world of Western Europe until about a century ago. Due to the Turkish conquest of the Balkans, scholarly activities of the native Serbian researchers were delayed until the late 18th-19th centuries.

A more systematic investigation of the documents containing information about Serbian musical activities and of Serbian contributions to the musical art began only with Stevan Mokranjac for folk music and with Kornelije Stankovic assembling melodies for religious services. Also one should mention Vladimir R. Djordjevic as one of the most significant collectors of folk musical instruments—as well as author of the first scholarly attempt at assembling data about Serbian musicians (Cf. his *Prilozi biografskom recniku srpskih muzicara,* 1950).

The true founder of Serbian historical studies of music was Kosta Manojlovic, who in the 1930s rediscovered the earliest example of a name of a Serbian musician in the 15th century—Kyr Stefan the Serb—found in a manuscript at the Monastery of Decani and since that time in several other musical manuscripts from that period. The renowned composer Miloje Milojevic was the first professional reviewer of concerts who educated musical audiences with his writings. Petar Konjovic and Vojislav Vuckovic, with their essays about various aspects of music, contributed to the discussions and further raised the standards of music appreciation among Serbs. A very distinguished role had fallen upon Stana Djuric-Klajn (1908-1986) whose activities included the publishing and editing of the extremely important musical journal *Zvuk* in the mid-1930s; later she taught the history of Serbian music after the founding of the Musicological Institute of the Serbian Academy of Science and the establishing of the Department for History of Music at the Music Academy in Belgrade. Both of these events took place in 1948. Since that time many students have graduated from the Music Academy.

An examination, as well as a thorough reading of the articles in this volume, will bring the feeling of pride to all Americans of Serbian origin. As a historian of music, it is my hope that this book will serve as an additional inspiration, a kind of impetus to all Serbian men and women in the US to record and preserve in writing (or on tape for an oral history) their memories of the activities in which they participated; to write down the names of friends and participants in these events, the names of songs they sang and pieces they played, especially if these were composed by their Serbian compatriots—*Da Se Ne Zaboravi* (So that it is not forgotten!).

In due time, we should be able to see an impressive collection of substantial data about singers, choirs, instrumentalists, ensembles, songs, symphonies, operas and other types of musical compositions that were created by descendants of Serbs who developed their talents in this country and demonstrated their artistry both as Serbs and Americans.

Many years hence, future generations will be looking at William Dorich's most impressive volume as the cornerstone of the Serbian-American library on music, and as the starting point of a renewal of interest in the preservation of our Serbian ethnic heritage.

Milos Velimirovic

**Milos Velimirovic**

Milos Velimirovic was born in Belgrade and studied violin since the age of six and piano from the age of twelve. In WWII, he joined the forces of General Mihailovich and, due to his linguistic abilities, was given the assignment of listening to all radio news broadcasts and preparing a daily bulletin of news. After a few months in the Avalski Korpus, he was transferred to the Press Bureau of the Supreme Command and with the Central National Council withdrew to Bosnia in the fall of 1944. Captured by Tito's army in April 1945, he was sent to the "Disciplinary Battalion" (euphemism for forced labor camp). Released from the army in 1947, he began his studies at the University of Belgrade (B.A., 1951 in the History of Byzantine Art). Simultaneously, he was the first student in the newly established Department for History of Music at the Music Academy (B. Mus., 1952 in the History of Music). Since 1952, Milos Velimirovic has resided in the United States. His graduate study was at Harvard (M.A., 1953; Ph.D., 1957). From 1957 to his retirement in 1993, Professor Velimirovic taught courses in the History of Music at Yale University (1957-69), at the University of Wisconsin in Madison (1969-73) and at the University of Virginia in Charlottesville (1973-93). His doctoral dissertation, *Byzantine Elements in Early Slavic Chant* (in 2 vols.), was published in 1960 in Copenhagen. He published seventy articles in scholarly periodicals and contributed more than sixty articles to several encyclopedias.

Memberships:
The International Musicological Society
The American Musicological Society
The Medieval Academy of America
The North American Society for Serbian Studies
The American Association for Advancement of Slavic Studies

# Introduction

Even though little evidence remains for Serbian music in the Middle Ages, a few documents do exist from Hilandar on Mount Athos—including the work of such important musicians as Kyr Stefan Srbin (Stefan The Serb). A rare document from the 13th century is the *Psalterium Bononiense*, written in Ravno near Ohrid. This collection of psalms has been of great interest to Slavonic scholars for some time.

The first Serbian musicians of the Middle Ages were the *skomrasi*—the equivalent of minstrels in the West. They were, at times, regular attendants in the medieval courts. St. Sava (1173-1235) used the word *spielmen* in his translation of *Ilovacka Krmcija* (Rule Book of Ilova). The word denotes a player, actor, dancer or musician. During Tzar Dusan's reign (1331-1346), there were documents that mentioned musicians by name for the first time—Preda Svirac (musician) and Hrusa Slepac (blind one).

The frescoes remaining in Serbian Orthodox churches in the Balkans reveal that music played an important role in the daily lives of the Serbian people. The frescoes painted in the Monastery of Lesnovo in the 14th century contain an illustration of Psalm 150 showing Serbians dancing the kolo with musicians playing in the background—a valuable piece of evidence attesting to the existence of music in the early Serbian culture.

After the Battle of Kosovo in 1389 and the destruction of Serbian nationhood, 500 years of Ottoman slavery ensued with the inevitable decline of the Serbian Orthodox faith and music. During this oppression, Serbs were forbidden to learn to read and write and were even compelled to invent a *silent kolo*—a dance without musical accompaniment, as instruments were also denied them by their persecutors. The only defenders of Serbian art and culture in these difficult centuries were the peasants who played the gusle, a one-stringed instrument used to preserve the history of the Serbian people through accompanying songs mourning their lost past. Over the centuries, thousands of these musicians were blinded as punishment by the pashas for singing of Serbian heroes. In this period large segments of the Serbian population moved north to Austro-Hungary—today's Vojvodina area of Serbia, where tamburitza music was born.

Over the decades, the western parts of the Balkans were influenced by Renaissance culture, while the Serbian side—under Turkish rule—was forced into a state of dormancy. Serbian culture would not reawaken until the beginning of the 18th century, when Serbs successfully threw off the bonds of Ottoman slavery, gaining their freedom and revitalizing their Orthodox faith and their music.

The most powerful figure in the 19th century in making Serbian folk poetry known to Europe was Vuk Karadzic, whose efforts resulted in Goethe's translation of many Serbian works. Goethe so loved the Serbian people, their poetry and their folklore that he learned to speak fluently in the Serbian language. Goethe was the major influence in encouraging Brahms, Loewe and Joseph Maria Wolfram to compose songs based on the Serbian folk poems and literature.

The formation of the Pancevo Church Choral Society in 1838 and the Belgrade Choral Society in 1853 resulted in each becoming centers for nurturing young talent. The first music schools were founded through the efforts of these choral societies.

The oldest Jewish Choir in the world is in Belgrade and was formed after the Jews fled Spain during the Spanish Civil War. The Serbs provided a hospitable environment in which the Jews resettled and prospered.

The brilliant work of Serbian composers like Bajic, Stankovic, Mokranjac, Marinkovic, Maksimovic, Djordjevic and Binicki accomplished in a hundred years what other cultures had the luxury of creating in several centuries. Therefore, the following pages are a testimony to those pioneers of Serbian music.

This book was inspired by the important work of Dr. Stojan Lazarevic of the Belgrade Choral Society, the research of Stana Djuric-Klajn, and the dedication of Serbians in the diaspora who maintained their culture and their music—at times under the most trying circumstances.

William Dorich

# The Death of a Guslar
### by Isidor Bajic (1878-1915)

In the west the sun has fallen
On the sheer stone cliffs,
Bursting into a myriad
Of precious stones.
And in the sky numberless
Stars begin to shine,
Just as on earth twinkle and glisten the
Tears of the sorrowing peasantry.
Why doth the peasantry
Shed tears so ceaselessly?
Topal Pasha has lain to bed,
But sleep will not come.
The pasha leaps, as he wipes his brow—
The devil tears at his soul.
A name of glory! A proud name,
For that does Topal yearn.
*"I hate wealth, I despise gold—
All is black and darkness.
Topal Pasha wants a song—
Wants a glorious name!
Gusle! Gusle! Rajo, rajo,
Those cursed bandits, brigands...
Must your name be glorified and sung—
You wolves of the mountains?
Should Topal harken to the song that
Eternity prepares for him?"*
Ah, but that pasha, Topal Pasha,
Has no such singer of his own.
This is the pasha madly shouting—
Torn by desire.
*"Ho, there! All Turks!
Prepare a manifestation of joy."*
*"Bring unto me the old man Mirko,
Why is he not here yet?
Bring unto me that guslar
With the divine strings.
Let him sing for me, let him glorify me,
Glory is divine.
Yesterday I put to death all four of his sons."*

The blind one sits clasping
His gusle to his bosom.
The Turks sing,
Shout all in rapturous orgy.
The Turks drink, Topal drinks not,
He thrusts away the goblet.
He strikes forward,
His steps all a tremble—
The blind man sits
Holding his gusle to his breast
His long grey hair falling
And covering his tears.
*"Avast, you Dog!
No, not that way, rather this,
My dear old timer."*
In whose hands lie the gusle
In him lies the strength.
*"Let me hear how sounds the glory
Of my greatness.
I will free from the dungeon
All four of your sons,"*
He lies.
Trembling, the blind man
Attempts to play his gusle.
A nauseating lump of his first utterance
Struck in his bosom, tears flow,
Wetting the gusle.
The guslar falls, menacingly shakes his
Gusle at the pasha, and dashes it to pieces
As he collapses and dies.
They have razed and destroyed
Our worldly goods—
They have harvested our hopes—
But the gusle, the Serbian gusle,
Knows not how to lie!

Guslar in Serbia
by Anastas Jovanovic,
National Museum, Belgrade.

# Serbian Composers
## from 1826-1938

### by William Dorich

Above:
Cover of the Mokranjac Liturgy,
Musica Sacra (Sacred Music),
Milan Bajsanski and Vojislav Ilic,
Prosveta Publishing, Belgrade, 1964, p. 8.
Courtesy of Archimandrite Dositei Obradovich.

**Milan Milovuk        1826-1883**
A self-taught musician, Milovuk was the first director of the Belgrade Choral Society. At the time, there were no Serbian choral compositions. Therefore, the choir sang foreign works—becoming a significant carrier of cultural Westernization. Milovuk opened the first private music school in Serbia and taught theory, violin, and cello. The first Serbian concert musicians were his graduates.

**Jovan Djordjevic        1826-1900**
Born in Senta, he was a teacher and a headmaster of several Serbian schools, and, for a while, he headed the Department of Education of Serbia. From 1863 to 1868 Djordjevic was director of the Srpsko Narodno Pozoriste (Serbian National Theatre) in Novi Sad. In 1868 he moved to Belgrade and became the director of the National Theatre. He wrote and adopted numerous plays. In an essay on Serbian theater published in the journal "Zastava." Laza Kostic, a famous Serbian poet, called Djordjevic "the father of the Serbian Theatre." In the summer of 1872, Milan Obrenovic decided to take over the power in the Serbian government that was held by a 3 member council (Ristic, Blaznavac, and Gavrilovic). Jovan Djordjevic was asked to write a play with historical-patriotic overtones. Djordjevic, a seasoned playwright at the time, and extremely patriotic himself, wrote a play in 2 parts called "Markova Sablja." The main characters in the play gave an overview of Serbian history in the previous 4 centuries. The characters were Kraljevic Marko, a fairy and a guslar. In a dream sequence, Kraljevic Marko is reminded by the guslar of the past victories and losses of the Serbian people—while the fairy talks about the bright future of the Serbian nation under Milan Obrenovic's rule. In order to emphasize a feeling of hope for the Serbian state and its people, in the last scene of the play, Djordjevic added a hymn based on his poem to the new knez called "Boze Pravde" (O God of Justice), which became the Serbian national anthem in 1904, after Jovan Djordjevic's death and numerous revisions.

# *Boze Pravde – O God of Justice*
## Serbian National Anthem

Words written by Jovan Djordjevic in 1872.
Music written by Davorin Jenko.
The anthem was officially selected by Serbia in 1904.

God of Justice; Thou who saved us
when in deepest bondage cast,
Hear Thy Serbian children's voices,
Be our help as in the past.
With Thy mighty hand sustain us,
Still our rugged pathway trace;
God, our hope; protect and cherish
Serbian crown and Serbian race!
Bind in closest links our kindred
Teach the love that will not fail,
May the loathed fiend of discord
Never in our ranks prevail.
Let the golden fruits of union
Our young tree of freedom grace;
God, our Master! guide and prosper
Serbian crown and Serbian race.

Lord! Avert from us Thy vengeance,
Thunder of Thy dreaded ire;
Bless each Serbian town and hamlet,
Mountain, meadow, heart and spire.
When our host goes forth to battle
Death or victory to embrace—
God of armies! be our leader
Strengthen then the Serbian race.
On our sepulchre of ages
Breaks the resurrection morn,
From the slough of direst slavery
Serbia anew is born.
Through five hundred years of durance
We have knelt before Thy face,
All our kin, O God! deliver,
Thus entreats the Serbian race.

The premiere of Djordjevic's play was held at the National Theatre in Belgrade on August 10, 1872. The music for the play was written by Davorin Jenko, a Slovene, who had moved to Belgrade and was active in the musical life of the city. The anthem was sung by Serbian soldiers in the Balkan Wars of 1912 and 1913 and again in World War I. Vojislav Janic mentions in "Zabavnik," a journal published for Serbian soldiers on Corfu, that the Serbian national anthem was sung in the churches, throughout Great Britain, to honor and to pray for the Serbian troops that brought the first victory of World War I on the Salonika Front, where 41,000 Serbs lost their lives in that battle along with 11,000 French, 4,000 Italians, 3,000 Russians, and 7,000 Americans. For celebrations of Vidovdan in 1916, 30,000 pamphlets with "Boze Pravde," translated by Jelisaveta Hristic, were distributed in England. Intonation of the Serbian anthem was very popular with the British people because it was similar to their anthem which was also a prayer to God for the monarchy. In the march composed in celebration of the unknown British soldier, the Serbian anthem's motif was used as the theme.

**Kornelije Stankovic 1831-1865**
Born in the Serbian quarter of Budim, he was a member of a Serbian family who settled there in the 17th century. Stankovic was orphaned at an early age. He went to live with his eldest sister, in Arad, finishing his elementary school education in Budapest—where he learned to play the violin and piano. Through Pavle Ridjicki, a wealthy landowner and friend of his father, Stankovic was helped with his education in Vienna in 1850. His first works were based on poems by Goethe and Schiller. Vienna at the time was considered the center of the Slav intellectual elite, its Serbian branch consisted of Vuk Karadzic and other writers such as Branko Radicevic and Jovan Subotic. In Vienna he wrote the first Liturgy, performed in the residence of the Patriarch Josif Rajacic in Vienna in 1851, and the second Liturgy, performed in the Greek Orthodox Church in Vienna in 1851. Although there existed various kinds of musical activity in Serbia and Vojvodina in the first half of the 19th century, according to the earlier historiography Serbian music was considered to have begun with Stankovic. He is the originator of Romanticism in Serbian music, particularly in his compositions for piano. His most famous works include, Tamna noc, Devojka sokolu i Siva magla, composed for singing and piano. Not only was he the creator of the Serbian national movement in music, he was a virtuoso musician who

Jovan Djordevic (1826-1900)

Kornelije Stankovic (1831-1865)

practiced 8 hours a day. Under the influence of Stefanovic, Karadzic and Fr. Raevskii, Stankovic studied folk songs and church music and published an anthology of church music entitled Pravoslavno crkveno pojanje. Through the Serbian folk themes used in his classical pieces, Stankovic introduced Serbian music to the West—in 1861 the Vienna Opera performed his work. His influence in the development of Serbian music is immeasurable. Two of his works, Rado ide Srbin u vojnike and Sunce jarko, were incorporated by Peter Ilich Tchaikovsky into the world famous March Slav written in support of the Herzegovina Revolt, 1875-1877, and called Nevesinjska puska.

**Davorin Jenko         1835-1914**
A Slovenian, he lived in Ljubljana, Vienna, and Belgrade. While not a Serb, Davorin Jenko was a major contributor to Serbian culture and Serbian music. He was the first director of the Slovenian Choral Society, founded in 1859. He directed the Pancevo Choir before coming to Belgrade. Jenko wrote Naprej zastava slave (Forward, Banner of the Slava), which later became the Slovenian National Anthem. In 1863, he accepted the post of choir master of the Serbian Choral Society. During the first years, he wrote choral compositions based on the texts of Serbian poets: Sabljo moja dimiskijo (My Damascus Sabre, after M. Popovic's poem) Sto cutis Srbine tuzni (Why are you silent, sad Serbian?, by V. Vasic) and Bogovi silni nasih otaca (The Mighty Gods of our Fathers, by D. Jaksic). In 1865 he became choirmaster of the Belgrade Choral Society as successor to Kornelije Stankovic, thus building a firm artistic base. Following Jenko, the choir was led by Marinkovic and brought to perfection by Stevan Mokranjac. After 1871, Jenko became the music director of the National Theatre in Belgrade. In the play "Marko's Sabre" by Jovan Djordjevic in 1876, the final choral song Boze Pravde (O, God of Justice) was later proclaimed as the Serbian National Anthem in 1904. He improved the classical Serbian Singspiel and, as the first author of orchestral music of a decent artistic and technical standard, Jenko paved the way for the Serbian opera. His achievements were acknowledged by his contemporaries and by Serbian society in general. Jenko was the first musician to be elected as a member of the Srpsko Uceno Drustvo (The Society of Serbian Scholars) and, later, a fellow of the Serbian Royal Academy.

Djura Jaksic (1832-1878)

Vladimir Djordjevic (1835-1939)

**Aksentije Maksimovic 1844-1873**
Born in Dolovo, he is among the musicians of Vojvodina who left a certain mark on their time. He was noticed for his very first choral composition Gde je Srpska Vojvodina? (Where is the Serbian Vojvodina?) based on the poem by V. Kacanski. The revolutionary character of this work resulted in his exclusion from the secondary school of Sremski Karlovci. Maksimovic subsequently devoted his abilities to the Serbian National Theater of Novi Sad, working both as kapellmeister and composer of many musical pieces for the plays then performed. Particularly popular even outside the theater were his songs Ej pusto more (Oh Wild Sea), from the tragedy Maksim Crnojevic by Laza Kostic, and Berberi su prvi ljudi (Barbers are First-classMen), from Kosta Trifkovic's comedy "Congratulations." Just when he began to acquire solid musical knowledge at the Organ School in Prague, Maksimovic died of tuberculosis.

**Dr. Jovan Pacu 1847-1902**
Born in Aleksandrovo near Subotica, he belongs by reason of his musical works (mostly arrangements for piano or paraphrases of folk-tunes) to the type of Biedermeier composers of a polished "salon" style and brilliant virtuosity. As a virtuoso pianist who began his career in Subotica in 1863, he gave concerts in Novi Sad, Vienna, Budapest, Osijek and many towns in Serbia and Vojvodina. Pacu was highly successful in Kiev, Russia, in 1885, where his concert program consisted exclusively of works by Slav composers—which contributed to his success. A physician by profession, he was active in politics of the day and published many articles connected with music. His compositions bear the unmistakable mark of the climate of the day; as for their themes, they sprang partly from actual political conditions, partly from the sentimental drawing room lyricism of the middle classes—Prag je ovo milog Srpstva (Threshold to Dear Serbia), Svetozaru Mileticu (To Svetozar Miletic), and Crnogorskom vojniku (To the Montenegrin Soldier). At the time, Pacu was considered one of the most important of Serbian composers.

**Mita Topalovic 1849-1912**
Born in Pancevo, his music was linked exclusively with his native town. He acquired his musical education at the Prague Organ School, like so many other Serbian musicians. Topalovic, as choirmaster of the Pancevo Choral Society, enriched its repertory and raised its artistic level. He contributed to the preservation and deeper observation of traditions introduced into that town by Nikola Djurkovic, as well as to the

Davorin Jenko (1835-1914)

Dr. Jovan Pacu (1847-1902)

high reputation not only of the choral society but also of Pancevo as the center of choral singing. Although he was a contemporary of Mokranjac and Marinkovic, he was closer to Jenko by reason of 2 main features of his works: by the lyrical and emphatically Romantic character of his melodies in such works as Oblaci (Clouds), Vetru s Kosova (Wind of Kosovo), Sokoli (Hawks) and Bojna pesma (The War Song). His solo songs; Pruzi mi pehar (Hand Me the Jug), O, pogledaj (Oh, Look) and Putnik (The Traveller) are composed in the style of belated Romanticism. They were very popular among Serbian basses.

**Josif Marinkovic          1851-1931**
Born in the Banat village of Vranjevo, he studied in Sombor and Prague before coming to Belgrade. His compositions embraced the new Serbian music movement of Kornelije Stankovic and techniques of Davorin Jenko. He was the director of the Belgrade Choral Society from 1881-1887. His career in music began when Belgrade was the capital of a small Serbian principality in the 1880s. By his death, Belgrade had become the capital of an entire new nation called Yugoslavia. Marinkovic remained consistently Romantic in style and he was the last eminent Romantic in Serbian music. Marinkovic's work originated several choral compositions, among them Pozdrav pevacima (A Greeting to the Singers), written on the occasion of the 30th Anniversary of the Belgrade Choral Society. Like other Serbian composers of the 19th century, he devoted himself mostly to choral compositions, for the numerous choral societies required that style of music. He was known for his particular regard for harmony. For the Serbo-Jewish Choral Society in Belgrade, he wrote the Worker's Song. Like the parallel between Bach and Handel that is drawn in West European music, the comparisons between Marinkovic and Mokranjac have been made in the history of Serbian music. His composition for voices and instruments entitled Cantata to Dositej Obradovic demonstrated his choral style of elaborate and monumental forms, by contrasting between soloists and choir and between individual dramatic episodes within the whole work, which sets Marinkovic apart from other Serbian composers. Josif Marinkovic was the first native Serbian to compose original music for the Serbian Orthodox Church.

WORKS:
Himna Balkana, (Balkan Hymn) Junacki poklic, (Hero's Battle Cry), Opelo (Requiem), Proletna zora (Dawn in the Spring), Povratak (The Return), Carju

Josif Marinkovic (1851-1931)

Stevan Mokranjac (1856-1914)

nebesni (O Heavenly King), Kosovaska humna (Kosovo's Hymn) and Oce Nas (The Lord's Prayer).

**Stevan Mokranjac          1856-1914**

Recognized as one of the most famous, if not, the most famous of Serbian composers, Stevan Mokranjac inspired the Serbian people and left them a legacy of music that will influence future generations. Many historical documents name December 28th, 1855 as the birth date of Stevan Mokranjac. However, this was the date reckoned by the old Orthodox Julian calendar—the difference between that and the Gregorian taken into account, the date of his birth is, in fact, January 9th, 1856. He took the name Mokranjac after the village of Mokranja, not far from Negotin, where his family originated. The line of Mokranjac's life and his work runs parallel with the rise of the Serbian middle classes and with the great political fermentations and dynastic changes which filled the last decades of the 19th century up to the First World War. More than any other musician of that time, Mokranjac was an integral part of his environment, whose basic tendencies found clear expression in his activity, both in his art and in society. The Realistic Movement, which reached Serbian literature through Svetozar Markovic, a preacher of the new social ideas, did not bypass Stevan Mokranjac, the young man from Negotinska Krajina. His significance in Serbian culture is evident both in the field of creation and in that of performing arts. He studied in Munich with Rheinberger, and, in Leipzig, with Jadassohn and Reinecke; in 1887 Mokranjac was president of the Society of Serbian Musicians. Under Mokranjac's leadership the Belgrade Choral Society gave concerts not only in all the larger towns of Serbia, but also outside its frontiers of those days—in 1893, in Dubrovnik and Cetinje, and in Skoplje and Salonika the following year. For this tour Mokranjac composed his first Rukovet on Macedonian folk motives (the 7th Rukovet). In the course of the same year, 2 concerts were given at Budapest—and they were a great affirmation not only of the Belgrade Choral Society but also of Mokranjac as composer. He wrote for that occasion Madjarske narodne pesme, a composition consisting of Hungarian folk songs for soloists and mixed choir. In 1895 the Choral Society sang in Sofija, Plovdiv and Istanbul, and at these concerts the choir achieved its greatest success. Mokranjac usually wrote compositions based on the songs from the region. On this particular occasion, he utilized the Turkish song Bircare si jok (Lover's Woes) as the base of his composition. The program, however, gave credit

Bozo Joksimovic (1868-1955)

Aleksa Santic (1868-1906)

to Mokranjac's pseudonym "Said Effendi," an obvious Turkish name as the fictitious composer—an example of his sense of humor and politics. He also wrote the first choral version of the Turkish national anthem Hamidija. In the summer of 1896 the choir had a grand tour of Russia, through St. Petersburg, Moscow, Nizji Novgorod, and Kiev, where their performances of works by Rimsky-Korsakov and Varlamov were particularly approved by Russian critics. The Choral Society had subsequent successes in Germany (1899), Bosnia and Herzegovina, Montenegro and Dalmatia (1910). The last concert tour under Mokranjac's artistic leadership took place in Rijeka, Trieste, and Zagreb. Mokranjac did not limit his work to the popularizing of music by means of choral singing only. In 1889 he founded a string quartet, whose members included Ferdinand Melher, Stevan Sram and Josip Svoboda, and which performed works from the classical as well as contemporary chamber music. He was the initiator and promoter of the League of Choral Societies (1903), and took part in the founding and subsequent work of the Association of Serbian Musicians (1907). Finally, in 1899 he founded, together with the pianist Cvetko Manojlovic and the composer Stanislav Binicki, the Serbian School of Music, of which he was director, also teaching theoretical subjects. Today it is called the School of Music Stankovic—Belgrade. His election as corresponding member of the Serbian Royal Academy in 1906 was an expression of public acknowledgment for his artistic achievements. He was also a member of the French Academy of Letters and Science. During the first Balkan war in 1912, Mokranjac became ill. In this period he wrote his last composition and conducted the choir for the final time. The second Balkan war began in 1913, and before his death he finished his last Rukoveti Zimni dani (Winter Days, to the poem by Jovan Jovanovic-Zmaj). Escaping the bombing of Belgrade, he found refuge with his family in Skoplje—where he died on September 29th, 1914.

WORKS:

He wrote 15 choral rhapsodies on Serbian and Macedonian melodies; the Liturgy of St. John Chrysostomos (published in Leipzig, 1901; an English translation as Serbian Liturgy was published after his death, London, 1919), Opelo (a funeral service); he also compiled a large collection of church anthems according to the Serbian usage and which derived from old Byzantine modes and wrote a collection of songs for mixed chorus, Rukoveti.

Stanislav Binicki (1872-1942)

Petar Stojanovic (1877-1957)

**Vladimir Djordjevic         1863-1939**
Born in Serbia, he was a composer of folk songs and songs for choir. He was a teacher of teachers, being the director of the Teachers' College in Jagodina for many years. He was a "melograph"—a collector of thousands of folk tunes and kolos. In the last few years of his life he devoted his time to music history and, upon his death, his entire music library was given to the Muzicka Akademija in Belgrade—where he held an honorary position of director of the music museum which he established.

**Bozidar Joksimovic         1868-1955**
Born in Svilajnac, he studied music in Prague and was one of the first in Serbia to compose an opera, Zenidba Milosa Obilica (Milos Obilic's Wedding)—which was never performed. He also wrote many works for orchestra, the overture Mladost (Youth, 1899), a Concerto for Violin and Orchestra (1930), suite Ugaseno ognjiste (The Extinguished Hearth, 1940), and symphonic poem Za cast i Slavu (For Honor and Glory (1943).

**Vladimir Djordjevic         1869-1938**
Born in Brestovac near Zajecar, he was remarkable as an explorer of musical folklore and as an historian. He is responsible for 2 collections of folk tunes from Serbia and Macedonia: Srpske Narodne Pesme—Kuzna Srbija, Serbian Folk Songs, 1928, with 428 songs, and Srpske narodne melodije—predratna Srbija, Serbian Folk Melodies, pre-war Serbia, 1935. These, along with 597 songs and the melodies and dances which Djordjevic arranged for the piano, violin or choir, are a useful source for the investigating of Serbian and Macedonian melodies for those interested in folk music, as well as for composers of arrangements—although his way of transcribing melodies is obsolete today. His publication of the Biographical Dictionary of Serbian Musicians and his attempt at making a bibliography of Serbian music were valuable contributions to the preservation of historical Serbian music.

**Stanislav Binicki         1872-1942**
Born in Jasinka, near Krusevac, Serbia, he was educated in Krusevac, Nis, the University of Belgrade and Munich's Music Academy. Composer, performer, pedagogue and organizer, he taught music in Leskovac and was a member of several choral societies—including Obilic and the first Belgrade Choral Society. His musical style is Romantic and in 1903, he wrote Na uranku, the first Serbian opera ever performed.

Petar Krstic (1877-1957)

Isidor Bajic (1878-1915)

He was also a founder of Akademsko Muzicko Drustvo (Academic Music Society) with the intention of developing and improving instrumental music and performances. He was director for the Military Ministry in 1904, formed the military orchestra, the first symphony orchestra in Serbia, which performed not only works by Serbian composers, but also famous pieces by renowned composers such as Beethoven and Haydn. He also wrote music for the Royal Guard. Binicki was one of the founding members of the Serbian School of Music in 1899 with Stevan Mokranjac and he was the founder and director of the Stankovic Choral Society—arranging numerous concerts through Serbia and abroad. In 1912 he produced Stevan Hristic's Resurrection for the first time. His religious compositions include a Liturgy for mixed voices. In 1920 he became first director of the Belgrade Opera. His wife, Miroslava, played piano accompaniment and conducted the choir. In the field of drama, Binicki composed the music for Periklova smrt, an opera, and Posljedni gost, a musical drama. His music for plays includes: Put oko sveta, Veselinovic's Djidu and Nusic's Nahod. Among his folk compositions, the Seljancica series of 6 songs based on the work of poet Milorad Petrovic is the most famous. His finest songs for chorus are Cini ne cini, Tri devojke and Divna noci. Of his songs for solo, Grivna Mijatovke and Da su meni oci tvoje were written in the spirit of folk music and were most successful. During WWI, Binicki withdrew with the Serbian army over the mountains in Albania into Corfu. His Mars na Drinu (March to the Drina), an ode to the First World War Serbian victory at Mt. Cer in August of 1914, has become a classic.

WORKS:

A requiem, a wedding service, and a thanksgiving service in Binicki's opus of religious compositions have an important place, but particularly important is his Liturgija (The Liturgy) and Opelo (Orthodox Requiem). His beautiful version of Oce Nas (The Lord's Prayer) remains highly significant to Serbian people. He also wrote Ekvinocio and Ljiljana i Amarila, (Operas).

**Petar Krstic                         1877-1957**
Born in Belgrade, he studied at the Vienna Conservatory with R. Fuchs. Returning to Belgrade, he conducted opera at the National Theatre in 1939 and became inspector of several music schools. He succeeded Davorin Jenko as music director of the National Theatre in Belgrade and became the director of the Stankovic School of Music. With less creative talent but more knowledge and better techniques than

Petar Konjovic (1883-1970)

Miloje Milojevic (1884-1946)

Binicki, Petar Krstic left a far greater number of works. This inevitably meant a wider variety of expression, but his work, on the whole, bears the mark of the Belgrade style as did that of his older contemporaries. After Mokranjac's death, he succeeded him as director and teacher of the Serbian School of Music and he spent the rest of his life actively participating in a variety of fields—as choirmaster, conductor, writer of musical criticism, editor of the musical magazine Muzicki Glasnik (Musical Herald, 1922) and as an able and diligent organizer who took part in public life. His many compositions for plays by native authors were, in fact, a preparation for Krstic's most important work, the opera Zulumcar (The Young Tyrant), after the play by S. Corovic, 1928. A few years before his death he wrote another opera, based on the folk ballad Zenidba Jankovic Stojana (Stojan Jankovic's Wedding), but it was never staged.

His work was based on Serbian national tunes, including the opera Zulumcar (Belgrade, March 23, 1927); Cantata jutro slobode (1919), several orchestral suites of national dances, choruses and songs. He edited a Serbian music dictionary and arranged the musical score to the National Theatre production of "Snow White and the Seven Dwarfs."

**Isidor Bajic**                        **1878-1915**

Born in Kula in Backa, he learned the elements of music at the Serbian secondary school in Novi Sad from Jovan Grcic, his teacher. He went to Budapest to study law, according to his father's wish, but registered at the Academy of Music instead and studied composition with Professor Hans Koessler. He returned to Novi Sad in 1901 to teach music at his former school. A very industrious, energetic and ambitious young man, he was active in many fields. In 1903 he founded Srpski Muzicki List (The Serbian Musical Journal), the only music magazine in Serbia at the time. He also founded Srpska Muzicka Biblioteka (Serbian Musical Library) which published his own as well as other composers' works. In 1909 he founded the School of Music in Novi Sad and carried on the tradition of "besede," conducting choirs and orchestras and writing text books for his pupils—The Theory of Singing by Note (1904) and Piano and Learning How to Play (1904) among others. Bajic composed many works in varied genres and forms—from opera to potpourris for orchestra and tamburitza. His compositions for piano are a part of his musical opus that were mostly influenced by European Romanticism, especially Franz Liszt and Peter Ilich Tchaikovsky. He wrote a great many songs composed for the plays Seoski lola (The Village Playboy),

Stevan Hristic (1885-1958)

Jovan Bandur (1889-1956)

Cucuk Stana (Tiny Stana), Divljusa (The Wild Girl), and Rakija (Brandy). One of his most important pieces of work was the opera Knez Ivo od Semberije, (Prince Ivo of Semberia, 1911), composed from Branislav Nusic's play. The closeness between the orchestra and the action of the play, as well as the expressive melodies of the vocal parts, contributed to the wide popularity of this opera. In the domain of original compositions the cycle of solo songs, Pesme ljubavi (Songs of Love), as well as the Album of Piano Compositions, are the works in which Bajic is most removed from folklore and where he reaches the highest level of individual expression as an artist. Isidor Bajic is best known in Serbian literature for his poem Guslareva smrt (The Death of a Guslar, shown on page 9). He used folklore to such a degree as a foundation for some of his compositions that, Jesen stize dunjo moja (Fall is Here, My Dear) and Zracak viri (A Ray of Light), are considered as folk songs.

**Petar Stojanovic               1877-1957**
Born in Budapest, in the same Serbian part of the town Buda where Kornelije Stankovic also came into the world, his father, Evgenije, was an enthusiastic lover of music, played chamber music with his sons at home and even composed, in an amateurish way, in the manner of Serbian National Romanticism. Stojanovic graduated as a violinist from the Budapest National Conservatory in 1896. He continued his studies in Vienna, graduating in composition. There he became known for his recitals and concerts of chamber music and gained a high reputation both as a performer and composer, in particular after his first Concerto for Violin and Orchestra (1903). Stojanovic also wrote at that time the lighter genre of comic opera in The Tiger (1906). But the next important affirmation of Stojanovic as composer occurred when he wrote his second Concerto for Violin and Orchestra, which was played for the first time by Jan Kubelik in Prague in 1916. He came to Belgrade in 1925, where he became director of the Stankovic School of Music. When the Academy of Music was founded in 1937, he became professor of violin and kept the post until 1945. He wrote mostly in the sonata form of compositions of chamber music; 5 sonatas, 3 sonatinas for violin and piano, string quartet, piano quintet, as well as his concertos; 7 for violin, 2 for viola and one for violoncello. Although Stojanovic composed operas and operettas, as well as some solo songs, he was above all a composer of instrumental music. Special recognition among those works belongs to the Second Violin Concerto, op. 30 (1912), the Fifth Concerto for Violin,

Kosta Manojlovic (1890-1949)

Ljubomir Bosnjakovic (1891-1987)

op. 78 (1944), and one of the last works of the old master, revised by new means of expression both in harmony and rhythm, based on the jazz idiom—the Double Concerto for Piano and Violin, op. 110 (1952).

**Stevan Todorovic         1882-1926**
Born in Novi Sad, he studied in Segedin, Vienna and Munich. In Belgrade, he founded and operated a tutition-free school of painting, voice and gymnastics. He was one of the founding members of the Belgrade Choral Society and its president and a vocal performer for 30 years. He also founded the Sokol organization in Serbia and organized the first public exhibition of art there. A prolific artist, he produced portraits, icons, historical works and watercolors, which appeared in Serbian ethnographic exhibits in Moscow. He also did magazine illustrations depicting the Russo-Turkish War of 1876-77.

**Petar Konjovic         1883-1970**
He studied at the Prague Conservatory with Novak and was choral director and teacher in Zemun and Belgrade from 1906-1914. Konjovic had many administrative and artistic tasks in Belgrade after the First World War. He was minister of education for the areas of Zagreb, Osijek, Split and Novi Sad and director and general manager of the opera in Zagreb. In 1920, he toured Europe as a pianist. From 1927-33 he was director of the national theaters in Osijek, Split and Novi Sad; from 1933-39, intendant of the National Theater in Zagreb. In 1939 he settled in Belgrade as a rector and professor of the Academy of Music. Without breaking with his predecessors, he gave new depth to the musical nationalism of the 19th century, writing in the modern musical idiom and relying on his own aesthetic principles which often became dogmas. He was an Impressionist in his style of musical expression and was mostly interested in composing operas. Although he had written his Symphony in C Minor, his Muzika duhovna (Religious Music, a collection containing 2 liturgies and several chants for holy days, composed before 1915 and published in 1938), Symphonic Variations na selu (In the Village, 1915), as well as many solo songs before the end of the First World War, the true musical character of Petar Konjovic was clearly shaped by the works he wrote between the 2 wars. His most important orchestral works include Na selu (In the Country) which originates from folk melodies through which his music evokes scenes from peasant life. Equally important are Makar Cudra and Jadranski capriccio (Adriatic Capriccio, for violin and orchestra).

Milenko Zivkovic (1901-1964)

Vojislav Vuckovic (1910-1942)

Konjovic's contribution to chamber music is considerable and is enriched by 2 string quartets and 2 suites for wind instruments. The most important place in his opus is occupied by the opera Miloseva zenidba (Milos's Wedding), Knez od Zete (The Count of Zeta), Kostana and Seljaci (The Peasants). One of the main characteristics of Konjovic's music is its enduring link with song and a preference for this form of composition developed when he was still a young boy and later at the Teachers' Training College when he conducted Rukoveti (Bouquets) by Mokranjac. Konjovic, more than any Serbian composer, came to learn music through songs and melodies and not through the simple formula of harmony usually learned in early piano lessons. At the age of 13 he composed songs without accompaniment, believing that the melody itself can be sufficiently expressive. It was at the Teachers' College that he composed his first operatic work and by the time he arrived in Prague to complete his musical studies (1904-1906) this gifted, self-taught artist, already had the finished score with him. Therefore, his chamber works and symphonic compositions are connected with song, originating from the concepts of the compositions. Another characteristic of Konjovic was his fondness for the larger forms. He used them more than any of his Serbian contemporaries.

Thus came his collection Lirika (Lyrical Songs), consisting of 24 songs and Moja zemlja (My Land) in 5 volumes consisting of 95 songs. Konjovic also wrote, Knjiga o muzici (Book of Music). After the Second World War he was elected a full member of the Serbian Academy of Sciences. Konjovic's opera Kostana, first performed in 1931 and revised in 1940, has become his most popular work. The most important sections and dramatic moments from this opera are included in the Simfonijski triptihon (Symphonic Triptych). Foreign critics once said of Kostana and Symphonic Triptych, that these were of "human significance, although constructed on a local theme of the Southern Balkans."

WORKS:
The operas Vilin veo or Zenidba Miloseva (The Wedding of Milos, Zagreb, April 25, 1917), Kostana (Zagreb, April 16, 1931), which included Kestenova gora (The Chestnut Mountain) and Velika cocecka (The Great Cocecka), Symphony in C (1908), Capriccio Adriatico, for violin and orchestra (1920), Knez od Zete (The Duke of Zeta, Belgrade, May 25, 1929), Makar cudra, symphonic poem after Maxim Gorky (1944), Muzika skrivenih slutnji (The Music of Hidden Forebodings), Vrgolan (The Urchin), Zagorski pejzazi (Zagorje

Landscapes), Tatko Stojanov (1948), Seljaci (The Peasants, Belgrade, March 3, 1952), 2 string quartets, solo pieces for violin, cello and piano, 24 songs, 100 Serbian folk songs, Moja zemlja (of which 25 are arranged for voice and small orchestra). He published a book of essays, Licnosti (Personalities, Zagreb, 1920) and a Monograph on composer Miloje Milojevic (Belgrade, 1954).

**Dr. Miloje Milojevic                1884-1946**
This Belgrade-born Serbian composer and writer of music was taught piano by his mother; then entered the Serbian Music School at Novi Sad. Returning to Belgrade after graduation (1904), he became a student of literature at Belgrade University and a pupil at the Serbian School of Music. His work differs in style, depending on where Milojevic was living at the time. While studying musicology in Prague, his work was in the style of Expressionism. In 1907, he married the singer Ivanka Milutinovic and they settled in Munich until 1910. His style was then Neoclassical. Milojevic served at the headquarters of the Serbian Army in 1914. From 1917-19 he resided in France where his style was predominately Impressionistic. Upon returning to Belgrade in 1919 his style was again influenced by Mokranjac and Serbian folklore. He published a school manual, Elements of the Art of Music (1922). As a composer, he wrote mostly in lesser forms: was influenced successively by Grieg, Strauss, Debussy, and Russian Modernists.

WORKS:
Piano suite, Grimaces Rythmiques (in the modern vein), was performed at the Paris Festival on June 26, 1937. His list of works contains 89 opus numbers. Among his dramatic works is The Death of the Yugovic Mother.

**Stevan Hristic                1885-1958**
Born in Belgrade, he studied in Leipzig, Rome, Paris and Moscow. Returning to Belgrade to become conductor of the National Opera Theatre, he also taught at the Music Academy, Belgrade. From the beginning to the end of his career he maintained a constant stylistic orientation centered on his belief in certain aesthetic principles which he consistently observed throughout his creative period. His Impressionistic style was very close to Ravel's. To better understand and improve his knowledge of religious music and to become better acquainted with its various styles, he went to Moscow in 1910—where A. Kastaljski assisted him in studying the Russian Church style. After that, he went to Rome and L. Perosi introduced him to the Latin polyphonic style. The result of these studies were his works Vaskrsenje (Resurrection), oratorio for soloists, choir and orchestra (to the text of the biblical drama by Dragutin Ilic) and his first Opelo (Orthodox Requiem) in E minor. With a group of musicians he founded the Belgrade Philharmonic in 1923 and was director until 1934. From 1924-34 he was director and conductor of the Belgrade Opera and was responsible for its flourishing period of enriched repertory. During this period, many eminent foreign artists—especially Russians—were featured in the opera along with the newly educated first generation of Serbian operatic singers. The repertory was particularly enriched by the works of the Slav classics and composers, Borodin, Dvorak, Mussorgsky, Rimsky-Korsakov, Tchaikovsky and Smetana and, by operas and ballets by Yugoslav composers, Baranovic, Binicki, Gotovac, Hatze, Hristic, Konjovic, Krstic, Odak, and Safranek-Kavic. When the Academy of Music was formed in 1937, Hristic, Petar Stojanovic and Kosta Manojlovic formed the core of the teaching staff. After the Liberation, his artistic activity was acknowledged by his election as a corresponding (1948), then full member (1950) of the Serbian Academy of Science and Arts—as well as by his being elected the first president of the League of Yugoslav Composers (1950). Although Hristic acquired his musical education in Germany, the German spirit hardly influenced his work. The melodies of his Symphonic Fantasy (1907), written with the great technical skill which is evident also in its orchestration, bear some traces of Bruch's Concertos, but they also have the Slav imprint. Such were his first works; however, everything Hristic composed after that was clearly marked either by the national style or by Impressionistic expression. Spanska pesma (The Spanish Song) to a poem by Vojislav Ilic, which he composed in 1949, has the characteristics of genuine Spanish folklore both in its rhythm and melody. It was almost as if Hristic wanted to be playful to show that he could compose in a Spanish style just as Ravel or Debussy. Among his works, his Opelo (Eastern Orthodox Requiem (1918), in B-flat Minor, ranks above all the others by the originality of its expression. By its masterful polyphony and by the depth of emotions, it equals Mokranjac's work of the same name.

WORKS:
Composed the music drama Suton (Sunset, 1925), a ballet, Legend of Ohrid (1947), and many choral works, Ponoc (Midnight) Vece na skolju (Evening at the Beach) and Jesen (Autumn) which became popular.

**Rikard Svarc                    1897-1942**
Was a Jewish composer and was killed in the Croatian concentration camp of Jasenovac. His artistic orientation was that of the most progressive and cultured musicians of his time. He studied at the Academy of Music in Vienna, studying composition with Joseph Marx. He enthusiastically followed the work of Schonberg and, upon leaving the academy, became a disciple of Alban Berg. His compositions, at least those which survived the Holocaust, reflect classical calm and austerity, but also the new, free breath of the Schonberg-Berg School. Those works are: Sonata for Violin in C Minor, Variations and Fugue on Mozart's Theme for the Piano, String Quartet, B Major, the ballad Na galiji (On the Galley, to V. Nazor's poem) for baritone and orchestra and Pet pesama (Five Songs) to Arabian poems. Rikard Svarc occupied the post of conductor of the Osijek Opera and Philharmonic, then was the head of the Music Department of the National Theater, and choirmaster and teacher in the School of Music in Split. He was one of the founders and editors of the magazine "Muzika" (1928-1929) and one of the most diligent musical critics of "Zvuk" (1932-1936) and "Muzicki Glasnik." He spent the last years before his death as director of the Isidor Bajic School of Music in Novi Sad, from where the Ustashi took him to Jasenovac.

**Jovan Bandur                    1889-1956**
A disciple of J. Marx in Vienna and J. Kricka in Prague, at first Bandur was more active as conductor than as composer. He was the first to perform in Belgrade with the Academic Choral Society Obilic, Stravinsky's Oedipus Rex, Szymanowski's Stabat Mater, Janacek's Eternal Gospel and Slavenski's Religiofonija. He was also conductor at the Belgrade Opera (1931-37) and choirmaster of the Pancevo Choral Society. His compositions between the two wars were written mainly in minor musical forms and showed his inclination toward the lyrical and emotional. He was influenced by Post-Impressionism and Slavic Impressionism. After the Liberation, Bandur spent the last ten years of his life on his sick bed. During this period he wrote many outstanding pieces of music—including his great trilogy of cantatas which interprets in the language of music the suffering under the fascist occupation Poema 1941, (The National Fight for Freedom), Jugoslavenska partizanska rapsodija (The Rhapsody of the Yugoslav Partisans) and the triumph of freedom won through battle, Raspeva se zemlja (The Whole Country Began to Sing), a song he composed for soprano, tenor and mixed choir in 1949—taking the words from the poem by Gvido Tartalja. He is remembered for Na grobu streljanih djaka (On the Tomb of the Murdered Schoolchildren), based on the poem by Desanka Maksimovic, a famous Serbian poet and based on the Nazi massacre of hundreds of Serbian pupils from the high school of Kragujevac in October, 1941.

WORKS:
Kisa, (The Rain), Mesecina, (Moonlight), a cycle of madrigals for male and mixed voice choirs—includes Dubrovacki madrigal (The Dubrovnik Madrigal), from the poems by Dzore Drzic, and Srednjovekovni madrigal, slovo ljubve, (The Medieval Madrigal, A Word of Love), to a poem by Despot Stefan, 1938. He also wrote madrigals from folk poems, such as Svatovski (The Wedding Madrigal, 1928), Makedonski aj, zora se zazori (The Macedonian Madrigal, Hey, the Dawn Came, 1951).

**Milenko Paunovic                1889-1924**
A leading composer of his period, he was no less talented than others, but his career was halted by a premature death. Paunovic was educated in Novi Sad and at the Leipzig Conservatory, in 1911. He spent the years until WWI teaching music at the Teachers' Training College of Jagodina. He joined the Serbian army as a volunteer and went with the army to the Salonika Front and from there to France, where he was engaged as a member of the orchestra of the Royal Guard by S. Binicki. Attracted by Richard Wagner's musical dramas during his studies in Leipzig, Paunovic tried to create a national genre based on Serbian tunes and historical events—which, in its essential qualities, would be similar to Wagner's dramas. As he was active in the field of literature from his earliest days, he wrote the text for his first musical drama—Smrt majke Jugovica (Death of the Mother of the Jugovici, 1911), a work from which only the overture has been preserved. His best and most powerful work was the first Yugoslav Symphony (1914) based on the work of Djura Jaksic (1832-1878), one of the most important Serbian romantic poets.

**Ljubomir Bosnjakovic    1891-1988**
He was educated at the Serbian School of Music in Belgrade and furthered his studies in Vienna and Berlin. Bosnjakovic was a graduate of the Conservatory in Naples.

works:
Selo moje ubavo (My Beautiful Town) and O, Moravo (Oh, River Morava). His Splets (Rhapsodies) from Lika, Herzegovina, Bosnia and Vojvodina are as popular as his Smrt majke Jugovica (Death of the Mother of the Jugovici). In 1961 he wrote the opera Robinje (Slave Woman), and in 1969 he wrote the very popular Vojvodjanke (Maiden of Vojvodina).

**Kosta Manojlovic    1890-1949**
Ethnomusicologist, musical author and critic, and choirmaster, he was a diligent organizer of musical life, actively taking part in many aspects of public life—Kosta Manojlovic approached all these fields with equal, almost romantic, enthusiasm. He acquired his musical education from Stevan Mokranjac in the Belgrade Theological School, from Miloje Milojevic, Stevan Hristic and Danica Krstic at the Serbian School of Music, and then continued his studies in Moscow (before WWI) and Munich, graduating from Oxford University in 1919. Among his first works was the psalm Na rekama Vavilonskim (On the Rivers of Babylon) for 2 mixed choirs, baritone and orchestra (1918), 2 Liturgies (1914-1915) and a cycle of solo songs, Jugoslovenske narodne pesme (Yugoslav Folk Songs, 1917-1919). These compositions were a musical transposition of the painful and tragic experiences of an enthusiastic young patriot who underwent all the hardships of the war. First dean of the Academy of Music in Belgrade in 1937, during his lifetime, he participated in investigative studies of musical folklore of Serbia and Macedonia with the Serbian Academy of Sciences and Arts—researching the origins of more than 2,000 folk tunes. In his devotion to Mokranjac, Manojlovic wrote Spomenica Stevanu Mokranjcu (In Memory of Stevan Mokranjac, 1923). He also edited Mokranjac's Opste pojanje (General Chant) in 1935, writing an extensive foreword as well as introducing into the collection those chants which Mokranjac did not have time to complete. He paid much attention to the history and problems of Church music, particularly investigating the similarity of the chant in various Eastern Orthodox nations and the connections between secular and Church folk tunes, returning often to this subject in his numerous studies. He wrote as musical author and critic for Pravda 1919-1920, Jugoslavenski Glasnik, 1930-31, Vreme, 1931-34 and occasionally in Srpski Knjizevni Glasnik, 1923-25, among others—and was distinguished by a continuous trait of emphatic patriotism, which was not limited to his narrower homeland but included the whole Slav south, the whole of the Balkans.

**Milivoje Crvcanin    1892-1978**
He graduated from the Conservatory of Music in Belgrade and continued his education at the Conservatory in Prague. In 1939 he became professor of Orthodox Liturgical Music and held this position until 1941. His compositions are defined as being in classical form.

WORKS:
Symphonic Variations Cantata, 1922 and 1923. His solos accompanied by orchestra or piano—Tuzna pesma (Sad Song), Noc (Night), Borac pao (Fallen Soldier), Anica cuvala ovce (Anica Watched the Sheep), Bre devojce (Little Girl), Opelo (Funeral Service) and his Tri duhovne pesme (Three Spiritual Songs for baritone and mixed chorus).

**Mihailo Vukdragovic    1900-1986**
He learned composition with Miloje Milojevic in Belgrade and with Karel Jirak and Viteszlav Novak—and conducting with Vaclav Talich in Prague. Vukdragovic devoted an enormous part of his creative and artistic energy to his professional public activities as conductor of the Choir Stankovic, then the Orchestra Stankovic, as conductor of the Zagreb Opera, of the Belgrade Radio Orchestra, and of the Belgrade Philharmonic. He was professor of theory and conducting at the Academy of Music and head of Radio Belgrade. He was first secretary of the League of Choral Societies of the Southern Slavs, president of the League of Culture and Educational Societies of Serbia, dean of the Academy of Arts, secretary general of the Association of Yugoslav Composers and president of the Association of the Musical Societies of Serbia. His work is marked by a mature mastery, particularly evident in skillful instrumentation and well-composed vocal parts and in the technically well-solved relations between various parts of a composition.

WORKS:
String Quartet in F Major (1929), Nocturne for Orchestra (1927), Symphonic Meditations (1939), Put u pobedu (Road to Victory, 1944), followed by the lyrical cantatas imbued with elements of folk tunes—Vezilja slobode (The Embroideress of Freedom, 1947), from the

poem by Branko Copic and String Quartet in A Minor (1945).

**Marko Tajcevic**            **1900-1984**
Born in Osijek, he studied in Zagreb, Prague and Vienna. In 1945 he was appointed professor at the Belgrade Music Academy. He is primarily a folkloric composer and is at his best in choral works derived from regional folk songs. The foundation of his work is folkloric, but it is contemporary and modern in its color. He is remembered for Vospoite emu (Sing Unto Him), and 7 Balkan Dances for piano are brilliant stylizations of Serbian melorhythms. Among his choral works are Dvadeset Srpskih narodnih pesama (Twenty Serbian Folk Songs). For male or mixed choirs, often composed in the polyphonic style, he was inspired by Macedonian folk motives. Quite apart from choruses inspired by folklore are the Cetiri duhovna stiha (Four Spiritual Verses, to David's Psalms), which are a synthesis of classical polyphonic technique and the Eastern Orthodox style in music; he also composed Liturgija (Liturgy). Among his important works are 2 cycles for piano, Srpske igre (Serbian Dances) and Balkanske igre (Balkan Dances).

**Milenko Zivkovic**            **1900-1964**
After graduating in law, he continued his studies in composition with Hermann Grabner at the Leipzig Conservatory and with Vincent d'Indy at the Schola Cantorum in Paris. He was director of the Stankovic Choir and conductor of the Orchestra Stankovic. He was secretary general of the League of Southern Slav Choral Societies and president of the Society of Composers in Serbia from 1945-52. He was dean of the Academy of Music from 1952-1960. His work Rukoveti Stevana Mokranjca (1957) is a very serious and thorough study of the harmonic, formal and inner characteristics of these classical works of Serbian choral music and is a very important contribution to our musical science. In 1958 he was elected corresponding member of the Serbian Academy of Science and Arts. He trained a large number of already recognized young composers, among them Silvije Bombardelli, Dragutin Gostuski, Dusan Trbojevic, Enriko Josif, Dusan Radic, Vlastimir Nikolovski and Vladan Radovanovic.

WORKS:
The Symphonic Prologue (1930), Symphonic Fragments (1951), a ballet suite Zelena godina (Green Years, 1935), Classical Suite for Flute and Strings, as well as dance suites based on folk motives Igre iz Makedonije (Dances from Macedonia), Oda bratstvu (Ode to Brotherhood, to K. Abrasevic's poem, 1956) and he also wrote 5 suites for piano, as well as a children's opera, Decja soba (Children's Room, to Desanka Maksimovic's libretto).

**Aleksandar Gavanski**            **1901-1972**
He was born in Stari Becej and studied law and music in Subotica, with a specialty in piano. After graduating he practiced law while directing several choirs before going to Belgrade. Between 1945 and 1949, Gavanski was the director of the Radio Belgrade Choir and the Serbian radio station where he conducted and performed over 100 compositions. He directed the Stankovic, Lola Ribar and Prvo Beogradsko Pevacko Drustvo choirs. He also directed Beogradska Saborna Crkva, the Cathedral Octet in Belgrade's Cathedral continuously for 5 decades. The octet sang Na Bogosluzenjima (At Worship Services) during Sunday liturgy and performed sacred music concerts touring throughout Yugoslavia, Austria, Germany and Switzerland. Aleksandar Gavanski composed a number of works for male chorus, including Veliko Slavoslovlje (The Great Praise), Velicit dusa moja Gospoda (Bless The Lord O My Soul) Velika Jektenija (The Great Litany) and Oce nas (The Lord's Prayer) for solo bass and male choir, which is still in popular use today in Serbia. He also composed Opelo and finished a Liturgy for male choir just prior to his death. In 1966 and again in 1969 with the male ensemble Hor Aleksandra Gavanskog (Aleksandar Gavanski Choir) he recorded Russian and Serbian sacred compositions for the German recording company Muller International.

**Svetomir Nastasijevic**            **1902-1969**
He studied engineering and architecture at the same time that he learned to play the violin. His works include the music drama, Medjulusko blago (The Treasure of the Medjuluzje, Belgrade, March 4, 1937); Djuradj Brankovic, a national opera from medieval Serbian history (Belgrade, June 12, 1940); and several symphonic poems and choruses. In his operas, he adopts the Wagnerian system of leitmotifs. To the field of chamber music he contributed 2 string quartets, several pieces for piano, violin and piano, and a great number of solo songs. He wrote 5 suites for female voice choirs and 8 suites for mixed voice choirs. He is also known for ballet, including Zivi oganj (The Living Flame, 1942) and music composed for motion picture sound tracks.

**Milan Bajsanski          1903-1980**
Born in Belgrade, he was a composer and director of the Belgrade Opera from 1945-1963. He also directed a number of amateur choirs in Belgrade during this same period. He composed mostly choral music and wrote numerous articles for various music publications. He recorded on the Decca and Marconi labels.

**Predrag Milosevic          1904-1988**
He studied at the School of Music in Belgrade, where his instructor in piano was Rajna Dimitrijevic and music theory was taught by Miloje Milojevic. He studied composing, conducting and piano at the Munich Academy of Music and the Prague Conservatory. He was choirmaster at the Belgrade Choral Society and conductor of the Belgrade and Novi Sad Opera. He wrote incidental music for the plays Hasanaginica (Hassan-Agha's Wife, 1927), Kraljevic Marko (Prince Marko, 1928), Zenidba Carli Caplina (Charlie Chaplin's Wedding, 1934), The Barber of Seville (1948), a String Quartet, solo songs, and a number of motion picture sound tracks.

**Milan Ristic          1908-1982**
He studied in Belgrade and in Prague under Habe. A prolific composer, he wrote mostly instrumental music; his style ranged from Neoromantic grandiosity to economic Neoclassicism. Some of his works are written in an explicit dodecaphonic technique; in some, he makes use of quarter-tones. One of the most enthusiastic promoters of modern trends in Yugoslav music, his pre-war style followed Schonberg's Expressionism. His last phase of work is influenced by Neoclassicism. His suite for 4 trombones was performed at the SIMC Warsaw Festival in 1939. There is no doubt that Ristic's familiarity with the polyphonic technique of Schonberg's type contributed to his becoming a composer with very skillful and elaborate composing techniques and a very clever use of counterpoint and quarter-tone system.

WORKS:
Six symphonies (1941, 1951, 1961, 1966, 1967, 1968); Violin Concerto (1944); Piano Concerto (1954), Suite Giocosa for Orchestra (1958): Symphonic Variations (1957); Burleska for Orchestra (1957); 7 Bagatelles for Orchestra (1959); Clarinet Concerto (1964); 2 String Quartets; Wind Quartets; Septer; Violin Sonata; Viola Sonata; 24 fugues for various instrumental combinations; and Suite for 4 Trombones in Quarter-tones.

**Ljubica Maric          1909-**
She studied in Prague and was a conductor for a period of time, then she took up teaching at the School of Music "Stankovic," subsequently lecturing at the Academy of Music. Her early compositions, in atonal and athematic style, include a String Quartet (1933), a Quintet for Wind Instruments (performed at the SIMC festival in Amsterdam in 1933) and Sketches for Piano. She wrote 3 folk songs for choir and Branko's Kolo for piano. Her artistic individuality drew the most noble inspiration from archaic and philosophical motifs, linked with the age-old deep roots of folk art. In addition to her Sonata for Violin and Piano (1948) and her solo songs Stihovi iz gorskog vijenca (Lines from the Mountain Wreath), she composed Vizantijski Koncert (Byzantine Concerto) for piano and orchestra (1959), the cantata Prag sna (The Threshold of Dreams) and Ostinato Super thema octoicha (1963), all from a great homogenous entity based on the 5 modes of the Oktoechos. The most important work of this composer is the cantata for a mixed choir and orchestra, Pesme prostora (Songs of Space, 1956). Original in its musical idiom, this cantata—which is one of the best works in our contemporary music—composed to the laconic inscriptions found on medieval Bogomil tombstones, reflects meditative depth and philosophical asceticism and is dramatically suggestive.

**Stanojlo Rajicic          1910-**
He studied music in Vienna and Berlin, and—upon returning to Serbia—joined the faculty of the Belgrade Academy of Music. Undecided between the careers of pianist or composer, he did choose composition and graduated from the Prague Conservatory. His early pieces are set in a radical idiom of atonal music, verging on dodecaphony, but later he adopted a national style derived from melorhythms of Serbian folk songs. In 1958 he became a full member of the Serbian Academy of Sciences and Arts.

WORKS:
2 operas: Simonida (Sarajevo, May 24, 1957) and Karadjordje (1973); a ballet Pod zemljom (Under the Earth, 1940); 6 symphonies (1935, 1941, 1944, 1946, 1959, 1957); 3 piano concertos (1940); 2 clarinet concertos (1943, 1962); Cello Concerto (1949), Bassoon Concerto (1969); Magnovenja (Moments); a song cycle for mezzo-soprano and orchestra (1964); piano trio (1943); 2 string quartets (1938).

**Djordje Karaklajic       1912-1986**
Devoting most of his creative abilities to folk songs, for which he wrote arrangements, he made a kind of rhapsody from various regions—Songs from Eastern Serbia, Songs from Gruza, etc., as well as composing arrangements of individual songs or dances (over 200 tunes for educational purposes), he arranged folk songs for children's choirs and for piano. A collector of songs and folklore, this musicologist compiled and published 27 books on songs of Serbia and Macedonia. In 1964 Djordje Karaklajic established and conducted the National Symphony, which concentrated on music inspired by national folklore. He was also the compiler and publisher of a book entitled Collection of Partisan Folk Songs, with N. Hercigonja in 1962.

**Oscar Danon       1913-1909**
Is a Jewish composer who was born in Sarajevo and now lives in Belgrade. A composer and choral director, Danon studied in Prague, obtaining a doctorate in musicology and aesthetics. From 1963 to 1970 he was professor at the Music Academy in Belgrade and director of the Belgrade Opera with whom he traveled extensively throughout Europe. Danon is best known for his choral work, Kozara (The Mountain Kozara) from the cycles Pjesme bore e pobjede (Songs of Battles and Victories). He was secretary of the Composers Union of Belgrade from 1950 to 1953.

**Vasillje Mokranjac       1923-1984**
He was born in Belgrade and was raised in a musical environment (his father was a cellist, a nephew of the famous Serbian composer Stevan Mokranjac). Vasillje Mokranjac studied piano and composition at the Belgrade Academy of Music. His early works are romantic in style, but he gradually began experimenting with serial techniques—while safeguarding the basic tonal connotations, leading to Neoexpressionism.

**Slobodan Zelic       1924-**
Born in Dalmatia and self-taught, he came to the United States as a young man and is currently the director of the Petar Krstic Choir in Steubenville, Ohio. He composed and arranged many beautiful songs such as: Moj dilbere (My Love) More moje Jadransko (My Adriatic Sea) Pesme sa plavog Jadrana (Song from the Blue Adriatic) Kosovski bozuri (Kosovo Poppies, 1986) A Jubilee Cantata, dedicated to the 600th Anniversary of the Battle of Kosovo, 1989).

WORKS:
Symphony No. 1 (Belgrade, February 2, 1962); Symphony No. 2 (Belgrade, April 1, 1996); Symphony No. 3 (Belgrade, October 25, 1968); Dramatic Overture (1950); Concertino for Piano, String Orchestra and Two Harps (Belgrade, March 15, 1969); chamber music; piano pieces; and incidental music for dramatic plays. He wrote Tebe Boga Hvalim (Psalm 149:1).

**Aleksandar Obradovic       1927-2001**
He was born in Bled and studied composition with Logar at the Belgrade Academy of Music, graduating in 1952. His advanced studies were with Lennox Berkley in London (1959-60). He traveled to Russia in 1963 and spent a year in the United States studying at Columbia University in the electronic music center in New York (1966-67). In 1969 he was appointed professor at the Belgrade Academy of Music. Formally, his music adheres to the architectonic classical design with strongly discernible tonal centers—but he experiments with atonal thematics and polytonal harmonies in some of his works and applies explicit dodecaphonic formulas.

WORKS:
A ballet, Prolecni uranak (Spring's Awakening, 1949); 5 symphonies: No. 1 (Belgrade, March 11, 1953); No. 2 (1959-61, Belgrade, January 22, 1965); No. 3 Mikrosimfonija for tape and orchestra (1967); Opatija (October 27, 1968); No. 4 (Belgrade, May 24, 1972); and No. 5 (1973); Symphonic Kolo (1949); Symphonic Scherzo (1955); Plameni vjetar (Flaming Wind), Song Cycle for Baritone and Orchestra (1955, Belgrade, January 13, 1959); Concertino for Piano and String Orchestra (1956); Concertino for Clarinet and String Orchestra (1958, Belgrade, May 26, 1959); Symphonic Epitaph for narrator, chorus and orchestra (1959, Belgrade, May 21, 1959); Scherzo-Overture (1959); Kroz svemir (Through the Universe), suite for orchestra (1961); Prelude and Fugue for Voice and String Orchestra (1963); Sutjeska for Narrator, Chorus and Orchestra (1968); Dramaticna Fuga for Wind Orchestra (1972, Belgrade, November 17, 1972); Quintet for Flute, Clarinet and String Trio (1950); Platani for Chamber Ensemble (1964); Microsonata I for Solo Clarinet (1969); Microsonata II for Solo Bassoon (1971); and choruses, songs and electronic pieces.

**Dusan Radic       1929-2010**
Born in Sombor, he studied at the Music Academy of Belgrade before going to Paris, where he had private lessons with Mihaud and Messiaen. His music follows

the cosmopolitan Modernistic manner, Baroque in formal structure, dissonant in contrapuntal intricacies and hedonistic in its utilitarian appeal.

WORKS:
Symphoniette (1954); Spisak (Inventory), song cycle of 13 numbers for 13 performers (2 female voices and 11 instruments, Belgrade, March 17, 1954); Balada o mesecu lutalici (Ballad of the Errant Moon), ballet (Belgrade, October 19, 1960); Concertino for Clarinet and Strings (1956); Sinfonia (1965-66); Piano Quintet; and several cantatas, songs, and theater music.

**Savatije Sava Ljubicic        1931-2011**
Born in 1931 in Cacak (Serbian Nashville) a small town in Serbia, Ljubicic was destined to shape his career at the age of three when he, at his father's music school, began to learn to play the accordion and just a few years later the piano. His father, a professional and successful country singer, has definitely shaped his son's life. While still in middle school, Ljubicic began to compose beautiful music.

*"The Secrets of My Life"* was a recently completed CD album just prior to his death. It sums up a versatile and successful career of this composer, who constantly surprises colleagues with his lifelong and tireless creative work. In Serbia, he issued 25 albums of Serbian songs and kolo dances, some of them performed by Yugoslav dance groups touring the world. In the easy listening genre, his ballads were sung by leading singers in the country. As such, Ljubicic received many honorable mentions, among them the prestigious **"Composer of the Year Award."** In the USA, Ljubicic continued to surprise by composing music in genres like: Latin, country-pop, gospel, classical, smooth jazz. Encouraged at UCLA by Eddie Manson, he also wrote film music and continued to unveil the secrets of his creative life. Almost immediately, his song *Bas Tamo* became an anthem of a Yugoslav American soccer team, while *Memories of the Adriatic,* expressed immigrants' longing for their homeland as well as their appreciation of America. Next followed a composition that revealed his own longing. Using some of his folk melodies, he wrote the *Yugoslav Rhapsody*, a classical composition that introduced the LA audience to the history of his country, to its heroic people, to its picturesque countryside and villages.

Ljubicic was especially proud of his song *L.A. That's You* that won him first prize in a USA song festival. Describing L.A., the song calls Los Angeles the "world's most dreamed of city." Still his latest *The Secrets of My Life* CD album is just another project Ljubicic kept hidden in his heart. It is an ethno-jazz oriented work that continues to unveil the composer's universal vision of the world. In 2011 at the Billboard's Song Festival, his composition *November* won him first place in the jazz category. Sava Ljubicic's music is a refreshing contribution to today's life. It is a blend of heart-felt melodies that in a romantic manner uncover the composer's universal sensitivity for people and for their environment.

**Vojislav Kostic         1931-2010**
Born in Belgrade, he studied in his native city and adopted the sophisticated style of utilitarian music. His Characters for Clarinet, Piano and Eighteen Percussion Instruments (1958) were performed many times in Yugoslavia. He also wrote a Divertimento for Wind Quintet and Suite for Bassoon, Piano and Ciganska prica (Gypsy Tale) for male chorus and chamber orchestra, to Gypsy texts (1964).

**Vladan Radovanovic           1932-**
Born in Belgrade, he studied at the Music Academy in Belgrade. His early works are set in a Neoclassical style; later, he annexed ultramodern techniques, including electronic effects. His Urklag for Mezzo-soprano and Chamber Orchestra (Belgrade, March 14, 1962) deploys a counterpoint of instrumental colors with the soloist singing wordlessly. Similarly wordless is his suite Chorales, Intermezzi e Fuga for Women's Chorus (Belgrade, May 16, 1992). His experimental period included such innovative works as Sphaeroon in 26 vocal parts, singing detached vowels (Belgrade, March 14, 1962) and Pentaptych, a suite for voice and 6 instruments (Belgrade, April 22, 1964).

WORKS:
His 26 compositions include: Trio for Flute, Horn and Clarinet (1975); Duo for Violin and Cello (1976); Orchestral Suite (1978); Sinfonietta No. 2 (1980); Fantasy for Piano and Orchestra (1984); Quartet for Violin, Viola, Cello and Piano (1986); Four Points of View for Violin and Cello (1991). His 15 choral compositions for mixed choir include: Srpski napjevi (1975); Starogradske pesme (1975); Pesme iz Makedonije (1977); Starogradske pesme (1986); Devojacki san (1989); Pesme sa Kosova (1992); Izvorne narodne pesme (1993) and Music of The Divine Liturgy with Supplemental Hymns (1978-1994).

**Zoran Hristic**  1938-
A composer who studied in Belgrade with S.T. Rajicica. For many years he worked as a free-lance musician in Modern Expressionism. He wrote works for both vocals and symphonies with more than 30 scores for motion pictures and more than 100 pieces for radio, television and theater. In 1973 he composed a ballet entitled Darinkin Dar (Darinka's Gift) based on a true story and Rodoslov (Genealogy).

The author gratefully acknowledge Slobodanka Boba Shaw for editing the Serbian language in, and adding relevant facts to, the Serbian Composers section. Mrs. Shaw sang for many years in the Belgrade Cathedral Choir under the direction of Aleksandar Gavanski (See p. 26).

*Serbia, valiant daughter of the Ages,
Happiness and light should be thy portion!
Yet thy day is dimmed, thine heart is heavy;
Long hast thou endured—a little longer
Bear thy burden, for a fair tomorrow
Soon will gleam upon thy flower-spread valleys,
Soon will brighten all thy shadowy mountains;
Soon will sparkle on the foaming torrents
Rushing toward the world beyond thy rivers.
Bulgar, Turk and Magyar long assailed thee.
Now the Teuton's cruel hand is on thee.
Though he break thy heart and rack thy body,
'Tis not his to crush thy lofty spirit.
Serbia cannot die. She lives immortal,
Serbia—all thy loyal men bring comfort
Fighting, fighting, and thy far-flung banner
Blazons to the world thy high endeavor,
—This thy strife for brotherhood and freedom—
Like an air-free bird unknowing bondage,
Soaring far from carnage, smoke and tumult,
Serbia—thy soul shall live forever!
Serbia, undaunted, is immortal!*

       Helen Leah Reed, 1916

"Serbian Villagers on Their Way to Exile."
(*Serbia A Sketch,* Helen Leah Reed,
The Plimpton Press, Norwood Mass., 1916, p. 113).
Courtesy of Archimandrite Dositei Obradovich.

# Music In The Feudal Era
## *Skomrasi—the First Feudal Musicians*—by Stana Djuric-Klajn

*A*t the period when the tribal system with its patriarchal culture was dying out and a new class-structured society was being formed and feudal estates established, between the ninth and twelfth centuries when the first states came into existence, the first signs of secular music culture can be traced through Church literature. After the Christian Church was established, one of its first tasks was not only to eradicate the remnants of pagan polytheism, but also to put an end to those deeply rooted profane manifestations which were opposed to the morals of the Church.

Evidence of musical professionalism in the Balkan states of the Middle Ages, similar to that in the West, can be found in Church literature. Wandering musicians, typical of the feudal era and known under various names in various countries, i.e., minstrel, jongleur, ioculator, etc., had their counterparts in the territory inhabited by Serbs and Macedonians.

Saint Sava,[1] in his translation of the *Nomokanon* (a codex called also Ilovacka Krmcija) already speaks about *spielmen,* (the word spielman denotes a player, dancer, fiddler or musician). There can be no doubt that this foreign word for the profession came into the Old Slavonic language along with the German performers. There were Germans in the mercenary army of the ruling dynasty of the Nemanjic, as there were among the crusaders who passed through the lands of the South Slavs. There certainly were also Serbs and Macedonians in that profession, proof of this is to be found not only in the existing Old Slavonic terminology of the Serbian version, but also in the fact that they have been mentioned quite often in historical documents.

The names for these musicians and their multifarious practices were mutually closely related and can be convincingly proven by an illustration in the respected 14th century novel entitled *Serbian Alexandrida*. The *Serbian Alexandrida* is a translation of Pseudokalisten's novel about Alexander the Great of Macedonia. That manuscript copy from the end of the 14th century was preserved at the National Library of Belgrade until the 1941 German attack on the city which destroyed the library and most of these documents. A preserved portion by a 14th century artist (shown here) illustrates four musicians painted in the lower part of the scene under the name of *"players"*—their instruments can be classified (from left to right) as types of small drums, psalteries (harps) lutes and *gusle*. In this case the role of the *"player"* is purely that of a musician, although it is very characteristic that another group of musicians in the same painting blowing horns (trumpets) bears the name of *praskarnici,* which clearly provides evidence that there was a Serbian word for the musicians with wind instruments in the Middle Ages.

*Above:* Banquet at Alexander's Court (Serbian Alexandrida, 14th century).

1) V. Jagic, Krmcija iovacka (a codex), Starine VI, pp. 60, 81-82. Grada za slovinsku narodnu poeziju, Rad JAZU 37, Zagreb, 1876. p. 73.

## "Woe to them who drink wine listening to the music of the gusle."

The illustration of the musical accompaniment at a feast discloses a custom of ancient origin in the courts of Serbian feudal noblemen and kings. The monk Teodosije (13th to 14th century), a Serbian, wrote, praising the virtues of the King, Stevan Prvovencani (Stevan the First-crowned)—that his various activities, among other things, used music *"to cheer the hearts of his lords while sitting at the head of the table, by playing on his drums or gusle, as was the custom of kings."*[2]

Players-entertainers in the capacity of *"praskarnici"* (blowers), *"skomrasi"* (actors), or *"sviralnici"* (musicians) were members of the staff of certain estates and feudal courts, but they were treated as the lowest rank in the social hierarchy of those times—just as were jongleurs and ioculators in Western Europe.

At the time of Tsar Dusan, the state was at the peak of its feudal power and it is then that many customs characteristic of feudal courts were introduced in Serbia (the court ceremonial modelled on that of Byzantium, titles etc.). Authority and rank in the hierarchy of the highly developed feudal system depended largely on possessions, which is to say, on the size and expanse of lands. Tsar Dusan's charter given in 1353 to Bishop Jacob makes a gift of the estate (the Church of St. Nicholas on the river Pcinja near Skoplje) along with all the material goods belonging to it—namely the men who work on that property. Dusan's charter specifically mentions, among others, *"free"* men, peasants and craftsmen, two slaves and, at the end, PREDA THE MUSICIAN and the BLIND HRUSA. According to the word attached to his name, Preda was no doubt a professional musician who had been working in that area (and this is the first known name of a Serbian skomrasi-player).

Priests and monks were strongly forbidden not only to take part in such entertainment but even to be present where they played or where there was dancing or satanic songs and ditties coming under the prophet's curse: *"Woe to them who drink wine listening to the music of the gusle."* Popular entertainment in the form of dancing and playing music was considered so immoral that it was forbidden to those who were about to get married, for they had to *"observe chastity."* That is why Teodosije, writing about St. Sava and exalting his moral and ethical virtues in the spirit of the theological view of the world, said that he avoided *"idle talk"* and hated the *"indecent and harmful songs of the young men, songs which lead the soul to final weakness."*[3]

And, yet, in spite of the strict moralistic Church proscriptions, the popular joy in music, dancing and acting and the professionalism in that field could not be bridled. Villagers gathered regularly for entertainment, as they do today, in places which were called *Igriste*—(dancing grounds).

*Above: Blind Bard*, by Risto Vukanovic,
National Museum, Belgrade.
2). Teodosije, St. Sava's Life, Old Serbian Biographies,
M. Basic, Belgrade, 1930, p. 191.
3). Teodosije, op. cit., p. 89.

The popular court entertainers of the day included DRAGAN FROM PRIZREN, who was in the service of the municipality of Dubrovnik in 1335. Such musicians were seen in the courts of Serbian and Bosnian kings and noblemen, and they also went to Dubrovnik to make the festivities of its patron saint, St. Vlaho, even more magnificent. They obviously traveled as organized companies, which certainly must have given mixed performances in which there was dancing, singing and acting—for they are mentioned in the documents of the Dubrovnik archives under various names: *tubatores* (trumpeters), piffares (fifers), *campagnatores* (bagpipers), *gnacharini* (drummers), and *sonatores* (musicians).

Serbian rulers most certainly kept company with musicians at their courts. Stevan Prvovencani, Despot Stevan Lazarevic (1370-1427) was one of the most cultured of Serbian rulers and during his rule, the *"School of Resava"* came into existence, the reformation of the language and orthography was carried out, the first root of historicism and the first humanistic ideas were established in Serbia. However, Despot Stevan did not neglect music—and that is why we see his trumpeters among those who were guest entertainers in Dubrovnik in 1408.

Besides its role of entertainer at court festivities and ceremonies, at popular gatherings and occasions for rejoicing, music was always a part of military exploits and triumphal celebrations. For Serbs (the Rascians) always went into battle accompanied by the sound of many instruments, especially the wind instruments. An anonymous Italian writer of the Middle Ages wrote that many battles were started by the signals of trumpets and subsequent victories were celebrated by music.

Apparent in the image below, music became acceptable to the Church as seen in this etching of a 14th century Serbian Church festival.

Kolo Dance, illustration of the Psalm 150 (Monastery of Lesnovo, 14th Century).

Church Festival in Free Serbia, *Travels in the Slavonic Provinces of Turkey-In-Europe,* G. Muir Mackenzie and A. P. Irby, London, 1867, p. 338.

# Church Music

by Stana Djuric-Klajn

Church music was practised with more continuity and system than the secular, being a part of the divine service and other religious ceremonies. It developed its characteristic features soon after the Christian religion was accepted in this region of the Balkans and after the Eastern and Western Churches became divided—a process which began in the 9th century. Ohrid was the cradle of literacy of Macedonian Slavs and the oldest cultural focus in the south of the Balkans. It was also the place where Church music was first studied and created. It is well known that two monks, Cirilo and Metodije (Cyril and Methodius), were spreading the enlightenment among the Slavs. They were sent by the Byzantine authorities to convert the Slavs to Christianity in order to consolidate the Byzantine political power over Bulgaria and Macedonia.

They had translated many religious books from Greek into the Church Slavonic language, which then used the Glagolitic alphabet. Among those works were the Oktoechos, as well as some other books containing Byzantine Church chants.

Their work was carried on towards the end of the 9th century by their followers, like Kliment and Naum who introduced the Macedonian language into the Church services and laid the first foundations of Macedonian literature. In the schools in which the priests were trained and lay people taught to read and write, Church singing was taught with great care. Special credit must be given to Kliment who worked all over the vast area of Ohrid Kutmicevica, as well as in the greater part of the Bulgarian Empire of that time. He trained singers among the priests at his school who equalled those in Greece in learning and musicality. On finishing Kliment's school, they spread the art of Church singing even further.

Being musically trained and educated, Kliment wrote the first canons, prayers and hymns in honor of individual saints. Among his other contributions to the Old Slavonic Orthodox music, he left us the first Penticostarion, that is to say a collection of hymns to be sung between Easter and Whitsun.

The Church of St. John the Divine, Lake Ohrid.

# Hilandar— The Center of Serbian Chant on Mount Athos

In the course of the 12th century the consolidation of political power and of the feudal system in the state of the Serbian ruler Stevan Nemanja occurred at about the same time as the strengthening of the influence of the Orthodox Church. Because power and influence were measured by the possession of estates and lands, the rulers built magnificent churches and endowed monasteries and churches with rich estates in order to have the clergy on their side in their conflicts with the serfs and enemies from other states. The agricultural production was highly developed, as labor was cheap owing to the exploitation of serfs. The exchange of goods was therefore possible to a great extent. Priests and monks thus enjoyed complete economic security and were able to devote themselves to spiritual and artistic matters. That is why we can find traces of the old musical culture in some monasteries.

The Monastery of Hilandar on Mount Athos with its 76 tenant villages was by far the richest. It was also an influential center of spiritual life not only of Serbs but also of other Orthodox peoples. From descriptions of life in the monastery we learn the first data on the Serbian chant. They were often quoted as a proof of the statement that there were two different kinds of chant in the Orthodox Church: the Greek and the Serbian. The source of the first piece of such information is the biography of Stevan Nemanja, by his son St. Sava and the second, Teodosije's biography of St. Sava. The monk Teodosije was a well known medieval writer (13th—14th century) whose main work was *Zitije Sv. Save* (Life of St. Sava).

Both works mention the fact that *"representatives of various nations sang in their own languages; one after the other, first at Nemanja's funeral, and, later, at the memorial service a year after his death."* Those two quotations, although indicative of certain differences, are not convincing enough as far as a distinctly Serbian chant is concerned. It is well known that there were monasteries of various Orthodox nations on Mount Athos (Serbian, Bulgarian, Romanian, Russian, and Greek). The monks from those monasteries could have sung each in their own language, but the chants must all have come from the same source.

However, according to other sources the Serbian chant as practised in Hilandar was neither Greek nor Serbian, but of the kind accepted all over Mount Athos which had a common root and various national variants. This was due to the Byzantine influence in the Balkans, as well as in Syria and Antioch. There is a confirmation of this in the *Psaltikija* of Stefan the Serb, who made a note—when quoting a Greek chant—that that was the Mount Athos way. On the other hand, Bulgarian historians say that there were the following singing schools on Mount Athos: Bulgarian, Russian and Serbian and that each of them brought into the singing their own musical characteristics, and even transcribed the songs in *"appropriate musical signs."*

Differences between the liturgical singing in various nations continued up to the 18th century, but they all had a common basis and there were mutual influences among them. The most convincing proof of this was provided by the Russian monk Vassilij Grigorovic-Barski, who spent some time on Mount Athos at the beginning of the 18th century and studied the way of life in all the monasteries. After stating that the Serbian monks in Hilandar were *"more-hospitable than all the others on Mount Athos, ... "* he adds that they say their prayers in the Slavonic language, but with a different, Serbian pronunciation. However, their way of *"singing, saying prayers and celebrating Vespers and Matins, as well as their way of announcing the service by clapper (simandron) is nearly the same as in all the other great renowned monasteries. There is hardly any difference, for they observe it (that way) thoroughly."*

But the Serbs, according to Barski, sing both their own and Greek religious songs, as the occasion requires: *"As a rule, they sing in their own Serbian modes in a clipped way, but on Sundays and holy days they sing Greek melodies in the Serbian language—their singing in this case is slow and very beautiful and that is the inexpressible beauty of the Church of Hilandar."* After visiting the Bulgarian monastery of Zographou, Barski was able to make comparisons—he says: *"It was a rule there, from the beginning up to my visit, to pray in the Slavonic language with the Bulgarian pronunciation, a little worse than the Serbian; their singing differed from the Serbian. "*

Egon Wellesz, one of the greatest authorities on Byzantine Church music, says, with regard to this: *"Byzantium did not play the leading part frequently ascribed to it. For, it is becoming increasingly clear that Byzantium was no more than a majestic meeting ground and a transit stop for all the creative forces, the origin of which is to be looked for further to the East; that the capitals of Asia Minor, Syria and Egypt with their background, hardly ruffled by Hellenic influence, must be regarded as true cultural centers. Owing to this, Asia Minor, Syria, Mesopotamia and Egypt are of primary importance for the arts of the Balkans; and then, the view that Serbian Church music was influenced by oriental songs or, as seems more likely to me, that it adopted them partially may be concluded from the constructive principle of the songs, which is of oriental origin."* (Aufgaben and Probleme auf dem Gebiete der byzantinischen and orientalen Kirchenmusik, Munster, 1923).

Although Barski spoke about the 18th century, his statements may be valid for earlier times, too—for he said himself that it had been like that *"from the beginning."* On the other hand, it is well known that life on Mount Athos did not change much with the passing of the centuries. Even today it represents a strange oasis with preserved remnants of times long gone by. Finally, the fact that St. Sava, on proclaiming the independence of the Serbian Church in 1219 (up to then under the ecclesiastic authority of the Ohrid Archbishopric) modeled the canons on those already existing on Mount Athos (which, in turn were modeled on the canons of the Monastery of Evergetide in Constantinople) speaks for a common origin of various ways of Church singing. After St. Sava built the Monastery of Hilandar, for which his brother, King Stevan the First-crowned of Serbia, supplied the funds, *"they made a set of rules concerning the divine service and singing, as was the custom then, and as they had learned in Vatopedi"* (a Greek monastery on Mount Athos). St. Sava later became abbot of the Monastery of Studenica and transferred to it his experience from Mount Athos.

*Left:* Unknown 20th century artist's rendition of Hilandar. *Middle:* The miraculous icon, *The Virgin Troyeruchitsa*, (the Virgin with Three Hands), is the most venerated icon at Hilandar. Painted in the mid-14th century, legend attributes it belonging to the icons painted by the Apostle and Evangelist St. Luke. *Right:* Aghia Sophia, Constantinople, the world's largest Eastern Orthodox Church was built in the 6th century A.D. During the siege of Constantinople in 1453 the church was confiscated and converted into a mosque. In recent years, as the Turkish nation continues to oppress Christians, Aghia Sophia has been converted into a museum, further alienating their Christian minority. (19th Century engraving courtesy of Basil W. R. Jenkins).

# HYMNS & *Surviving Manuscripts*

## by Stana Djuric-Klajn

Hilandar was the focus of Serbian culture in the Middle Ages, especially of literature, and it was also one of the first centers where Church singing was taught. Nearly all Serbian writers from the Middle Ages speak of Church singing on many occasions, but they do not mention the authors of those songs. Yet, we should remember that in Byzantium the men who wrote the verses were nearly always also composers who set them to music—and were therefore called poetsmelodoi. It is not impossible that St. Sava, too, did some work as a composer, editor of religious songs, or as translator of certain stichera from Greek books.

A similar supposition concerning the authorship of religious songs can be made with regard to Patriarch Pajsije, (16th century), a great "book lover" and a very cultured man who took care to preserve and save from annihilation many books and manuscripts scattered about in various monasteries. He himself was a writer. Patriarch Pajsije says in one of his works, "Service to Tsar Uros," he put in it "troparion" and "kontakion"—writing first the stichera of the small vespers ... "all in the order required by liturgy."

A sticherion is a church hymn by which a certain saint or a holy day are celebrated; it is sung together with some lines from the psalms and other parts of the Bible.

John Koukouzeles is the most significant name in the older Slavonic-Byzantine history of music. His work is very closely connected with the development of Macedonian and Serbian music. There are many controversies and unconvincing data concerning his work, his life, even the century he lived in, in the earlier musicological literature. This was caused by the fact that the earlier authors relied mostly on hagiographic literature, that is—literature based on legends of the lives of saints. However, certain facts can be reconstructed with some certainty. Drac, under the Archbishopric of Justiniana Prima, in present day Albania, has been mentioned most often as his birthplace. Dzermenci, near the Macedonian town of Debar, has also been mentioned. Koukouzeles was born in the 13th century, and lived about 80 years. He was exceptionally gifted in music. In numerous documents he has been described as "angel-voiced." His mother sent him to Constantinople to acquire a greater proficiency in music and in the Greek language. Koukouzeles became a court singer in the Byzantine capital, and he was appreciated for his outstanding wisdom and musicality—he chose to be a monk and went to one of the communities of Mount Athos as a hermit and domestikos (teacher of singing).

Kontakion copied from an illuminated medieval manuscript still in use on Mt. Athos. Courtesy of Basil W. R. Jenkins.

The creative work of Koukouzeles is nearly as important as his reformation of the theory of music and of musical notation. His compositions bear the mark of Byzantine music insofar as they are vocal monodies, but they differ from Damascene's chant—prevalent up to his time—by the introduction of ornaments and of wide, sweeping melodies. In addition to his original compositions, Koukouzeles worked on many existing Byzantine hymns, "improving" them by adding melismata. Koukouzeles' most mentioned composition is the "Lament of a Bulgarian Woman" (Polijelej na bigarkata). He composed it, according to the legend, imitating the melodic flexions of the voice of his mother who grieved over his departure. Among his other compositions is Pridvorna heruvimska pesma (The Cherubic Hymn).

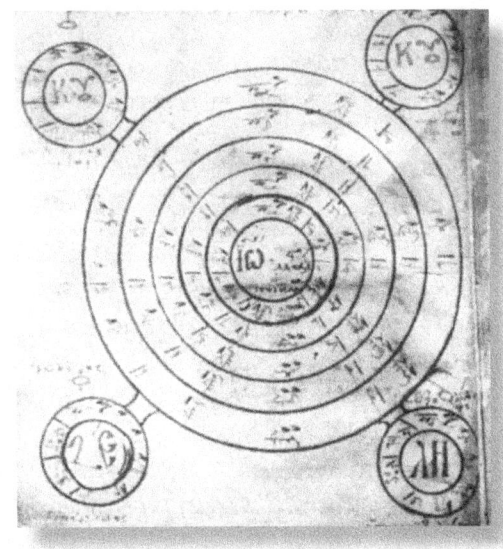

Veliko Iso papadakijskog poganja (The Great Ison of Papadikian Chant) is in fact a kind of solfeggio, a textbook for singers. Koukouzeles utilized a great many novelties in singing technique and in the modulations which are difficult to execute, even by the very skilled. This work was generally referred to as the "whip for singers"—and only good singers were capable of singing his compositions. Among many novelties by which Kokouzeles had enriched and refreshed Byzantine music was the "Papadikian" way, characterized by its wide melodic scope.

In the field of composition Koukouzeles was a revivalist and reformer, but in the field of musical notation he was more than a reformer. He founded a system of musical writing which existed up to the beginning of the 19th century called Koukouzeles' or the new Byzantine neumatic notation.

Many melodies of Serbian, Bulgarian and Greek Macedonian origin were put down in writing in Koukouzeles' notation, up to 1814. The significance of Koukouzeles' work as teacher, reformer and theoretician was made more evident by the fact that the following remark is often found in late Byzantine manuscripts: "The art of singing and the musical signs for it, with the whole cheironomy and composition were created by Master John Koukouzeles." The system of concentric circles for the study of modes has been ascribed to him, but we find it also in the work of the "Domestikos" Stefan the Serb.

During the Turkish occupation of the Balkans, from the end of the 15th to the beginning of the 19th century, Church music did not develop; it stagnated, remaining on the basis provided by the Byzantine music during the period when it had reached its peak in the Middle Ages. Original, creative work in music and musical literacy became very rare with the passing of time. Church music was reduced to the performance of Prosomoia, or singing of texts to melodies similar to those already existing. This practice led to many improvisations on the part of singers, to greater freedom in the interpretation and, in particular, to the introduction of elements of folk or secular music into that of the Church. It led also, however, to a complete loss of written music when music was passed on to future generations by oral tradition.

But the Serbian chant expanded, along with the migrations of the people, northward, to Hungary and, to a certain extent, to Russia. This chant was very close to that of Kiev or the old Russian way. The Serbian chant reached those parts thanks to the monk and writer Grigorije Camblak. From the 15th century on, the Serbian chant was sung in the Church of Southern Russia as well. Among the examples of Serbian liturgical music in Moscow there is a Serbian koinonikon, Pricastni stih (Communion Chant), from 1652. The walls of monasteries and churches, although often greatly damaged, give us a clear idea of the magnificent painting of that time. Under layers of chalk and mortar we still find old masterpieces that the enemy could not destroy.

Above: Graphic presentation of modes, *"Psaltikija"* of Stefan the Serb, 15th century.

However, evidence of musical creation is not only rare but, even if found, it is sometimes impossible to transcribe. The country was frequently devastated and ruined by hostile armies, but the loss of many musical documents of Serbian or Macedonian origin was also caused by the negligence and lack of understanding on the part of those whose duty it should have been to safeguard the cultural works of the past. The number of documents that have been examined, or deciphered and subsequently published and made accessible to us nowadays, is even smaller.

One of the rare surviving documents of music from that distant time is the Psalterium Bononiense, written in Ravno near Ohrid in the 13th century. Its name comes from the place where it has been preserved. This collection of psalms—which has interested Slavonic scholars for a long time—has not so far been subjected to musical research, although it presents an interesting example of the fusion of the ecphonetic and palaeobyzantine notations. The anonymous author of that Psalter was probably one of the followers of Clement's school.

The Psaltikija (Anthology) of the "domestikos"

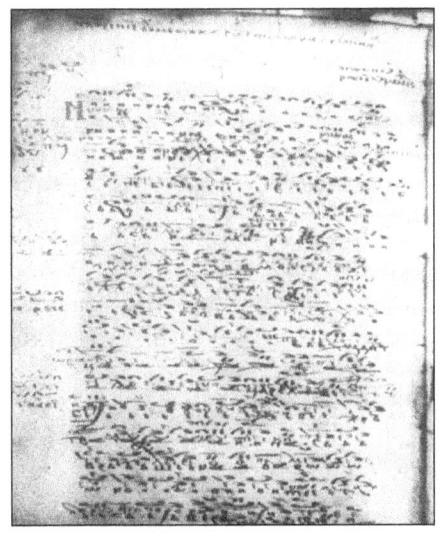

*Above:* Beginning of the Cherubic Hymn Psaltikija of Stefan the Serb, 15th century. *Top right:* Same music with modern notation. Transcription by Dr. Dimitrije Stefanovic. The original discovery of the work of Stefan the Serb was by the late Kosta Manojlovic (1890-1949). Professor Manojlovic was the first dean of the Music Academy in Belgrade, founded in 1937. Just prior to the German attack on Belgrade in 1941, Manojlovic had photographed several of Stefan the Serb's manuscripts. The Germans destroyed the National Library and only these priceless remnants remain.

STEFAN THE SERB played a significant role in Serbian musical culture. Unlike other manuscripts, mostly anonymous or of Greek origin, this one takes us back to its author, a man of Serbian nationality. The original of that manuscript under No. 93 in the catalogue of the National Library of Belgrade was lost forever on the 6th of April 1941, when the National Library was bombed and burned to the ground. Of this anthology consisting of over 300 folios, only 12 photographs have been preserved and they are kept in the Archives of the Serbian Academy of Sciences and Arts in Belgrade under No. VII/433.

This was a collection of liturgical chant with texts in Serbian and Greek written in late Byzantine notation. The first pages contained theoretical instructions or explanations of the signs for dynamics and intervals and their names in Greek and in the Church Slavonic languages. Moreover, there is the graphic presentation of modes in Koukouzeles' concentric circles—a scheme which the singers had to learn (Dorian-hypodorian, Phrygian-hypophrygian, Lydian-hypolydian, Mixolydian-hypomixolydian) with a special sign for each pitch of octave. (Shown on the previous page).

The collection contained 9 Serbian hymns. The most valuable among them are Ninja sili nebesnije (Now the Celestial Powers) and Vkusite i vidite (Taste and See), because both were signed by the author. Prior to the discovery of this fact, one could only try to guess who that first Serbian composer was. The only thing that was clear was his nationality and profession—"domestikos." In the Byzantine terminology that meant the man occupied himself with music. Stefan lived in Smederevo in the 15th century. He was in the service of Despot Lazar Brankovic—not only as "domestikos" but also as a "dijak" or copyist of other manuscript collections. He may also have illustrated them. Being a choirmaster, Stefan may have composed his own works. As for his using Greek texts, this is easily explained by the fact that there were many Greek emigrants in the Serbian Despotdom, for they had fled before the Turkish invasion. The Greek princesses lived also at the Serbian court—and, no doubt, the court choirs had previously sang in the Greek language.

Owing to the usual style of writing in the Middle Ages, many significant and interesting texts can be found on the margins of old manuscripts. They are sometimes more valuable than the text around which they were written. There are complete histories among them and they represent important documents for historians of future generations. From the marginal notes of this anthology, we see that it was used by native priests or monks, because there are frequent instructions or explanations above or beside the text about the manner of singing. On one of its pages an anonymous admirer of those songs wrote: "Blessed be he who wrote this divine book…"

Although all sources or, rather, places where old and original Serbian manuscripts may still be stored (monasteries, old libraries abroad, etc.) have not been thoroughly searched, new documents about the past history of Serbian music may still be hidden. So far, those manuscripts or the names of their authors are unknown.

Thanks to the research work of Dr. Milos Velimirovic, to whom we are infinitely grateful for writing the preface to this book, we learned of the, so far, oldest composer of liturgical melodies—Joakim The Monk and Domestikos of Serbia, as he signed his work in 1453. The manuscript is now in the possession of the National Library of Athens (No. 2406).

Three compositions from that large collection bearing his signature are two Koinonika (Communion Chant) and a Theotokion (Hymn to the Blessed Virgin). Although Joakim's nationality cannot be established with full certainty, because the text under the neumes was Greek (and his title of the "domestikos of Serbia" need not necessarily mean that he was a Serb), still, this discovery proves once more the existence of close links between the Byzantine and Serbian Churches.

We learn from the same source that there is another manuscript (No. 928) in the National Library of Athens in which are mentioned the names of the hieromonk Nikola The Serb and Isaija The Serb, both from the 16th century, besides Kyr Stefan—of whom we have already heard. Isaija wrote Polyeleos Servikos, verses of Psalms 134 and 135 in Serbian Church Slavonic, as well as in Greek, while Nikola was the author of the Cherubic Hymn, with Greek text.

The Servikon, an anonymous fragment of Serbian chant, also from the 16th century, was found by Dimitrije Stefanovic at the Bodleian Library in Oxford (MS E.D. Clarke 14, AD 1553). This manuscript is particularly interesting because the text of that sticheron, dedicated to the Blessed Virgin, was written in Serbian Church Slavonic, but in the Greek alphabet.

Research work and studies of the old Serbian liturgical chant began, on a wider scale, around 1955. Thus we may hope that more "newer" works of the old "domestikoi" will be found and that they will help in reconstructing, approximately, the past, and in repairing that which had been inaccessible and hidden for centuries, owing to the harsh course of history in this area of the world.

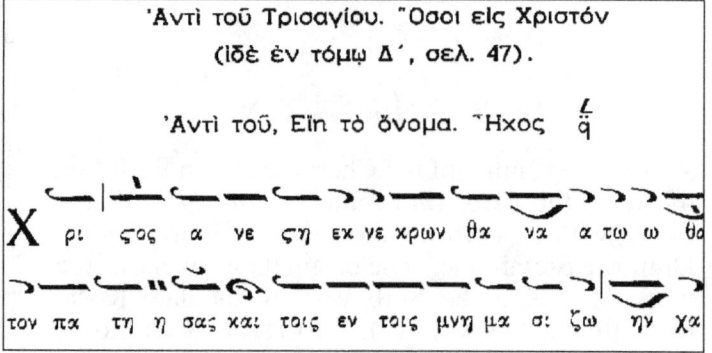

Byzantine music notation from the 1600s, translated in 1841 by Konstantinou 1st., who was a cantor. The music is Christ's Resurrection Troparion, sung at Easter by the Serbian Orthodox Christians as *"Hristos Voskrese" (Christ Has Risen From The Dead)*.

# Serbian Musical Life in the 18th Century

## by Stana Djuric-Klajn

The Turkish domination lasted for 5 centuries and was characterized in the Balkans by its oriental feudalism—the first signs of the awakening of a certain bourgeois musical culture appeared in Serbia and in Vojvodina in the 18th century. When Eugene of Savoy—the leader of the Austrian army—drove the Turks from Austria and Hungary, he gained that victory by taking Belgrade in 1717. The Turks not only left the city of Belgrade, but also a part of northern Serbia. Owing to this, Serbia, particularly Belgrade, acquired new Western features during the Austrian domination from 1717 to 1739. The visible appearance of the city and the way of life changed, as well as the educational system which was entirely under the direction of the Orthodox Church. Many new schools were opened—some of them were German and Latin, with Roman Catholic missionaries from Austria as teachers. Some were local schools in which reading and writing were taught by newcomers from Greece and Russia.

Due to the efforts of the Serbian metropolitan bishop in Belgrade, Mojsije Petrovic, who wanted the Liturgy service to be presented in an eloquent and beautiful manner, "Daskal," or teacher Gerasim, the "old man" Konstantin, as well as the Greek, Nikola Logijatat, were brought to Belgrade. But, it was the famous and "experienced" singer Anatolije, a hieromonk from Mount Athos, who was most responsible for the great improvement in the art of chant. From his school for "psalm chanters" came the young men who had learned to sing "according to the Greek psalmody." Jovan Rajic, the author of religious books, complained in his writings of this period that the "Greek chant has spread everywhere and the Serbian chant has disappeared almost completely and is hardly to be heard anywhere nowadays."

1) D. Popovic, *Srbija i Beograd (Serbia and Belgrade)*, Belgrade, 1950, p. 219.

In these schools, where the teaching of reading and writing was primary, Church singing and chant was learned by repetition; the pupils did not even understand the text, as it was in Greek.

But the second generation of Anatolije's pupils wrote the Serbian Church Slavonic words under the Greek melodies. That is how two kinds of chant developed.

The Roman Catholics living in Belgrade during this period had a much more elaborate religious life—primarily because they were given financial help by the Austrian authorities. After the Austrians came to Belgrade, most of the mosques were turned into Roman Catholic churches. The colonies of Roman Catholic Dubrovnik people, scattered all over the Balkans, had their own churches in bigger cities. Those churches were mainly in the hands of Jesuits and Franciscans. Thus, J. B. Tavernier, among other foreign authors, writes in his notes in 1675 that he "heard a midnight mass with very beautiful vocal and instrumental music in a Dubrovnik church in Belgrade." Therefore, it is possible that there were organs in Belgrade at the time.

Instruments have never been introduced into the Serbian Orthodox Church. Secular music in Belgrade under Austria was almost exclusively in the hands of the occupying forces, in particular in those of the commander in chief of Serbia, Alexander of Wurtenberg. When this playboy officer—with qualities and inclinations typical of that period—gave balls in his "Ballhaus," all the distinguished citizens were ordered by the Burgermeister to attend these entertainments—famous for their splendor. The entertainment included light music, dancing and theatrical performances all done in the German language. Yet, "in spite of all the gaiety in the hall, they (the Serbs) were terrified—for they were likely to be put into chains

At the time of Maria Theresa and her successor, Franz Joseph I, Vojvodina was caught up by the same wave and spirit of French culture which was echoed in Croatian regions on the eve of the national movement known as Illyrism. The more prosperous groups of Serbs had adopted many customs and manners of the Austrian and Hungarian aristocracy and accepted many expressions of the culture brought from the country of Louis XIV. The minuet, that typical dance of the French *"golden age,"* in its triumphal sweep across Europe, did not pass by the periphery of the Austrian Empire, the Serbian Vojvodina.

Serbian lyrical poetry of the 18th century truly reflects the life of that society, giving us abundant information about the spiritual climate, inclinations and the way of life of the Serbian bourgeoise in general.

In addition to the French influence, Italian music and poetry had also some influence on Vojvodina toward the end of the 18th century through the Serbian officers of the army who took part in the war in Italy. Jakov Ignjatovic, a romantic Serbian writer of the day, said: *"In those songs, there was a whole legion of Venuses, Amors, Phyllises and Chloes, Marces and Dianes."* The tunes to which those poems were sung, of Dalmatian origin perhaps, were so widespread and popular among the people that they survived till the middle of the 19th century. They were superseded, owning to the political circumstances, by patriotic and belligerent songs of the Serbian people.

The ways and customs of the middle class upstarts, who adopted indiscriminately all that was *"distinguished"* and foreign, were turned to ridicule some time later by the Serbian playwright Jovan Sterija Popovic. He showed them not only in his comedy *Pokondirena tikva* (The Conceited Upstart), but also in his collection of articles Milobruke—in which he criticized the ways and customs of the society of Vojvodina at that time. As for learning and music, he said something very similar to a remark of an anonymous poet: *"At one time it was a great shame for a girl not to know how to spin, weave or how to knead bread ... but nowadays she is ashamed to do these things, and wants only to be a virtuoso on the fortepiano."*

Music was highly appreciated in Vojvodina, judging by the poetic evidence of it. The education of the middle classes, especially that of the young girls in towns, included unfailingly playing on some instruments. At that time (18th century), the harp was very popular—just as a century later the *"strumming on a guitar"* became fashionable. The printed catalogue of Emanuil (Emanuel) Jankovic's book shop in Novi Sad shows what music was played and what compositions were bought by the local customers. In addition to the number of books, especially works by contemporary French authors, that same catalogue quotes the printed music sheets which could be purchased there. These were mostly chamber duos, quartets or compositions *"a plusieurs instruments"* by Stamitz, Geminiani, C. Bach, Haydn, Paisiello and many others. Jankovic, who was a writer and an educated man, would certainly not have kept those works in his book shop if there had been no demand for them in Novi Sad, or rather, if there had been no inclination to play intimate chamber music in those circles.

The musical art of the people, resulting from specific national conditions of the life of Serbs, was in vivid contrast to that light-minded art of the Vojvodina of the 18th century, framed by rococo garlands, and inspired by Paris, Vienna and Budapest. The most outstanding example of folk art was the famous *"Academy of the Blind"* in Irig.

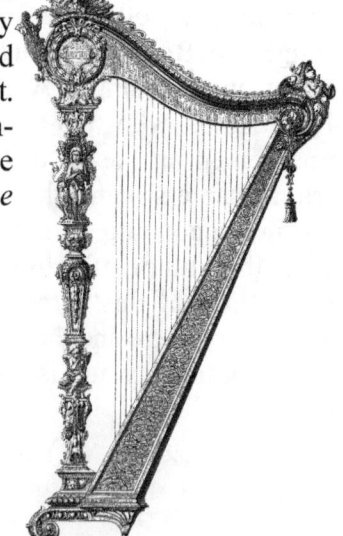

Although that was no academy or officially organized school in the true sense of the word, it was a center where guslars from Srem, as well as those from more distant parts, gathered. They had a kind of guild in Irig. Some of them were really masters of their art, and many other blind men came to learn from them. A fortress of the Serbian despots in the 15th century and in the 18th century the economic center of Srem, Irig was the town in the vicinity of the monasteries of Fruska Gora with the greatest number of inhabitants—and, therefore, was very convenient for furthering the traditional art of the guslars. Those blind men, and most Serbian guslars were blind, because they would not revere the pashas in their songs, rather, they would praise the Serbian heroes, hence the pashas would blind them as a punishment.

The Austrian authorities put an end to that "school" in 1780—because its national and political influence was opposed to the official policies of the state and because it produced many eminent guslars. Vuk Karadzic put down in writing the folk ballads he had heard from some of them. Vuk Karadzic (1787-1864) is one of the most important figures of Serbian culture of the 19th century. Reformer of the Serbian language and a collector of Serbian folk-poems, Karadzic was a linguist, ethnographer and historian —considered the father of modern Serbian literature.

At this important time, the renewed art of Serbian chant was born within the walls of the monasteries in Vojvodina—especially in Krousedol where the archimandrite was Dimitrije Krstic (1762-1843). Although he knew the Greek chant well, he paid special attention to the old Serbian chant and, combining the two, created a new kind of liturgical chant according to his own taste. By doing this, Krstic had not only trained new experts and teachers of singing—such as Jerotej Mutibaric (1799-1858) and Dionisije Cupic (1775-1845)—but he also established the chant known as the Karlovci Chant, which was later edited according to the instructions of the Metropolitan Bishop Stratimirovic and was, from then on, regularly practiced in that form. However, it was Kornelije Stankovic who later put it down in musical notation.

It is evident that a musical tradition developed in the drawing rooms of the intelligentsia, aristocracy and great landowners, as well as in the Church and among the people. The middle class lyrical poets left a great number of poems sung to melodies, the authors of which were as anonymous as were the poets themselves. As the Liturgical chant, it was transmitted exclusively through oral tradition.

The only example of written and, no doubt, originally composed melodies exists in Zaharije Orfelins' (Zacharias Orphelin) Pozdrav Mojseju Putniku (Address to Mojsej Putnik). This paper of 33 pages, published in 1970, is kept in the University Library of Wroclaw, Poland.[2] From the literary point of view, this manuscript is important for the fact that these were the first poetic lines of the eminent Serbian author of the 18th century—rather than for its artistic value. But it is even more interesting because of its graphic and calligraphic aspect—and, for us, for its musical content.

Dimitrije Stefanovic transcribed the festive ode, written on the occasion of the consecration of Mojsej Putnik as bishop of Backa in 1755, and there are musical signs in the Russian square notation from the 18th century in several places, accompanying the verses. These are either hymn endings of lines or refrains which follow the various verses. Other melodies are original, fundamentally close to the music as known in the towns of Vojvodina—the tune of that hymn is similar to the well-known liturgical song, to the tune of the first mode in the Hymn to the Blessed Virgin.

Several pages of the manuscript are decorated with ornamental elements of a musical character: there are many angels from whose bugles emerge the words "dostoin," "Vivat," etc.

There are also groups of musicians and choirs carrying in their hands things which look like posters with the same acclamations written across them. Although Orfelin did not sign the musical text (as he had not signed the illustrated parts of the manuscript), and has so far never been mentioned as a composer, we may assume, with some certainty, that the melodies were composed by him too. As for his time and environment, he was a man of extraordinary erudition and talents—a writer, enlightener, calligrapher, engraver, biographer and admirer of Peter the Great and critic of the parasitism of the monks.

He may have had some contact with music and acquired a certain knowledge of it on the occasion of his prolonged stays in Venice, Vienna, and Budapest, if not in his own country. We may therefore consider Zaharije Orfelin, the editor of the first Serbian magazine—"*Slaveno-Serbski Magazin,*"—as one of the first composers of Vojvodina.

With new waves of migrations northward to Hungary and Austria, Serbian culture found refuge in Vienna and Budapest. The migrating groups went that far to the north up to the middle of the 19th century—but after the fall of Absolutism, in the sixties, the migrants gradually receded back to their natural ethnic territory, the Vojvodina and Serbia.

Although at that time the charred homes in Serbia were still smoldering, its society was making preparations for a great transformation. Owing to the migrations, however, the first Serbian folk songs were printed in Vienna at that time—in modern notation and not in the old neumes.

## Serbian Music In the Bourgeois Society

When the Austrian troops left Serbia in 1740, the country was once more shaken by renewed Turkish aggression. This meant, of course, a return to the social and spiritual life of oriental primitivism. The little which had been achieved toward bringing Serbia nearer to enlightened Europe was again destroyed. While Karajordje's liberating wars may have brought temporary national freedom—it cost an enormous number of lives. Economic conditions in the completely ravaged country excluded any thoughts of the kind of higher superstructures which the art of music represents. Elementary forms of literacy had to be undertaken from scratch, but even that was not easy to achieve: *"For, at that time, there was no trace of any school in Serbia and every youth who wanted to learn anything had to go to a priest or to a monastery,"* said Archpriest Matija Nenadovic in his *Memoirs*.

*Above:* Serbian folk song printed in Vienna, 1815.
*Left:* 19th century engraving courtesy of Basil W. R. Jenkins.

There were 6 songs which Vuk Karadzic published in 1815, in the second volume of Serbian Folk Ballads; the notation and harmonization were by the Polish musician Franciszek Mirecki (1791-1862). Those songs have a historical and artistic value. When compared with Mokranjac's harmonizations of the same songs, it became evident that Mirecki had given a faithful transcription not only of their rhythm and melodic structure, but had also achieved the right harmonization for them.

A powerful figure of the 19th century, Vuk Karadzic who revealed the beauty of Serbian folk poetry to Europe, managed to interest Goethe in it; this resulted in Goethe's translating some of the ballads and in his urging many composers, from Joseph Maria Wolfram (1827) through Loewe up to Brahms, to compose songs after the Serbian folk poems in his own or in someone else's translation.[3] The interest in folk art, so characteristic of the romantic period, also prompted Emanuil Kolarovic from Sremski Karlovci to collect "almost a hundred different Serbian songs and to write them down in musical notation," as we learn from the magazine "Letopis Matice Srpske" (in 1828) which promised to publish them. Ten of those songs were indeed published in 1828, issue IV, but the remaining 90, which would be valuable for us today and would help in assessing what alternations they underwent in the course of time, were not published or preserved.

3). P. Slijepcevic, Uticaj Geteov na Prve Kompozicije Nasih Narodnih Pesama u Njemackoj (Goethe's influence on the first Compostions in Which Serbian Folk Poems Were Set to Music in Germany), Nova Europa, March 1932; Dr. J. Milovic, Goethe i Srpsko-hrvatska Narodna Poezija (Goethe and Serbo-Croat Folk Poetry), Filozofski Fakultet u Zadru, 1958, pp. 79-81.

# Music During the Reign of Prince Milos

by Stana Djuric-Klajn

Milos Obrenovic (1815-1839), founder of the Obrenovic dynasty.

The first published folk tunes merely hinted at the existence of a modest musical culture, but it is only during the rule of Prince Milos that we can speak of a more active musical life. In the first period of his rule, Serbia was an exclusively agricultural and primitive country where the wealth was amassed in the hands of a single owner—Knez (Prince) Milos himself. As the ruler of Serbia he maintained all authority, all the lordship and became the absolute master of Serbia and one of the richest men in the Balkans. With all his authority, Milos ruled not only the political life in Serbia, but the culture as well. The music of that time was in the hands of Turks and Gypsies and was therefore of a completely oriental character. The *"vizir's music"* played in Belgrade at the time was observed by Joakim Vujic, who, as a cultured European with Western education, said that he *"did not like the concert of that music."* It consisted of two violins, a pair of cinelli, a drum, a cimbalon, a tambourine and a triangle, on which a squinting Gypsy woman beat with an iron rod—*"all those instruments cannot, I am sure, make a musical concert such as our European instruments can,"* reported by Joakim Vujic.

That Turkish band inevitably accompanied the prince on all occasions, even on his Sunday outings up to the reform carried out by Josif Slezinger.[1] Among those musicians, the one who had a widespread reputation was the famous *"oberlautar"* Mustafa—who played the violin and *zurle* (a sort of oriental clarinet). He composed many songs and was able to entertain foreigners with his music, even though they were not particularly fond of Turkish music.

Although Mustafa and his company remained in Serbia to delight the people and the courtiers, the year 1831 was a turning point in the musical life of Serbia. Wishing to make the life of his court equal to that of other European rulers, Prince Milos decided to establish an orchestra of European instruments and professional musicians. He, therefore, summoned Josif Slezinger—who had been living in Sabac (1829), organizing the musical life of that town and teaching the children of Jevrem Obrenovic (Milos's brother). Slezinger was already well known as a man to whom pupils were sent in order to *"master the art of music."* Slezinger, born in Sombor in 1794, had musical practice rather than a thorough musical education acquired while playing in many orchestras of the Central European aristocracy.

1). Ami Boue, *La Turquie d'Europe, II,* Paris, 1840, p. 286.

He played many instruments (the violin, clarinet, horn, trumpet, etc.) and was the chief of the city orchestra (kapellmeister) in Novi Sad before coming to Serbia. When Slezinger came to Kragujevac, then the capital of Serbia, in 1831, he was given a task which was by no means easy. He was ordered to teach music and the playing of various instruments to men enlisted from the people, who were often illiterate, and was therefore forced to create his own teaching methods, to write arrangements and original compositions for that orchestra and to conduct it as well.

That *"Band of the Serbian Prince"*—as the orchestra was officially named—was obliged to play on festive occasions such as welcoming the prince and his suite, on state and Church festive days, at balls, military parades and every morning *"at the prince's rising and at sunset."* But the most important role of the orchestra consisted in taking part in the performances of the theatre newly founded by Joakim Vujic, and later administered by Atanasije Nikolic. On these occasions a choir was sometimes added to the orchestra.

The performances were preceded by a musical overture, and the orchestra also played during the intervals, as well as in the course of the performances—when, as was often the case, there was singing or the playing on some instrument incorporated in the play itself. For such plays Slezinger arranged the music of other composers, according to his needs and his orchestra, wrote vocal or instrumental versions of folk music and composed original music for some plays. That is how a specific genre of musical literature in Serbia originated—the so-called *"play with singing"* (a kind of local Singspiel). That genre was in favor with nearly all the Serbian composers of the 19th century. Among the plays for which Slezinger composed music are Joakim Vujic's *Snajderski kalfa* (The Tailor's Apprentice, 1835), J. Sterija Popovic's *San Kraljevica Marka* (Kraljevic Marko's Dream) and *Srazenije na Kosovom Polju* (The Battle of Kosovo), Atanasije Nikolic's *Ajduk Veljko* (The Outlaw Veljko), *Kraljevic Marko i Arapin* (Kraljevic Marko and the Arab, 1824), *Zidanje Ravanice* (The Building of Ravanitsa), *Zenidba Cara Dusana* (Tsar Dusan's Wedding, 1840) and *Smrt Srpskog Knjaza Mihajla* (Death of the Serbian Prince Mihailo, 1869).

The most interesting among all those plays was *Tsar Dusan's Wedding* (performed for the first time in Kragujevac in 1840). The contemporary newspapers acclaimed the *"premiere"* as a highly successful performance of a work *"composed of songs in the manner of Italian operas,"* adding that the *"whole play was set in musical notation,"* and stating later on, when the play was performed for the second time, that it was an *opera*. The surviving fragments of the piano score, however, show that the actors had to work on musical parts more than in other plays. Apart from the choir, seven characters in the play had singing parts and the orchestra also had their own purely instrumental items. Still, these are somewhat more extensive musical parts in an otherwise spoken text rather than an opera in the true sense of the word.

*Wedding Procession of the Emperor Dusan* by Paja Jovanovic (1859-1957), National Museum, Belgrade.

Above: Guslar player in Serbia by Anastas Jovanovich,
National Museum, Belgrade

# The Belgrade Choral Society 1853-1953

By Dr. Stojan Lazarevic

> By the middle of the 1800s, Serbian choral singing was popular in Serbia and throughout Europe.
>
> In the late 1870s, Serbian immigrants, fleeing Balkan oppression, brought the choral movement with them to America. This process continued through two world wars as tens of thousands of Serbian refugees fled to these shores. Through the years, numerous Serbian church choirs, choral societies and tamburitza musicians have maintained the Serbian culture and the Orthodox faith through music. Since 1936, the Serbian Singing Federation has arranged an annual festival in keeping with these ideals (see pgs. 62-63).
>
> In 1953, Dr. Stojan V. Lazarevic wrote the following history of the Belgrade Choral Society on the occasion of its centennial.

Serbian music has deep roots in the centuries-old past—and of all art forms—it occupies a singularly splendid role in the life of the people.

Whether it is folk songs for pure entertainment and dancing or a cappella choirs for the Serbian Orthodox liturgy, music is central to our history and culture. Unfortunately, the development of Serbian classical music was thwarted by the centuries of Ottoman dominance.

Because of that, the origins of Serbian classical music date from the early 1800s and the era of new-found Serbian independence.

With the independence of Serbia in 1830, the conditions were right for the return from Austria's Vojvodina of many Serbs whose forefathers had fled Serbia in the Great Serbian Migration of 1690. When they returned from Austria and Hungary, they brought with them the elements of Western urban culture, the social customs of Europe's cities of the 1800s. This group of Serbian intelligentsia became an unusually important cultural and political factor which influenced all aspects of Serbia's social development.

In Serbia the increasing economic strength, and the appearance of an urban intelligentsia at the uppermost levels of society led to huge spiritual and political changes in the entire Serbian society.

With their Western European educations and sophisticated ideas, this very group, especially between 1875 and 1900, formed the basis of the young and active citizenry of independent Serbia.

Due to the formation of this urban elite, Serbia was introduced to European classical music and witnessed the development of a Serbian national classical music of its own.

These Serbs, who came to Belgrade, brought with them from Vojvodina the idea for a Serbian national theater and choral societies. In fact, it was actually in Vojvodina that the first Serbian schools of classical music were founded.

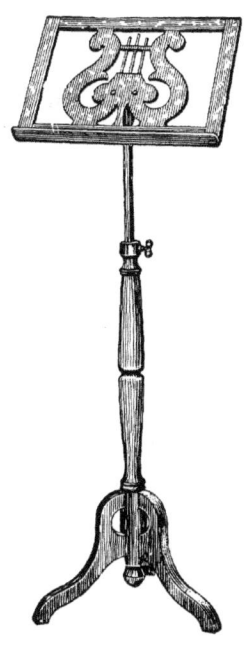

57

Belgrade emerged as an important commercial city—its cultural institutions also developed to keep pace with its wealthy merchant and artisan classes.

The Belgrade Choral Society did not happen all by itself. Founded on the 2nd of January in 1853, it reflected the specific social and political conditions which Serbia faced at the time. Like all similar groups, it served the narrow goals of its members, as its original statutes show. Their stated goals were entertainment, personal enjoyment and training in music.

The Society intended to spread European classical music to the widest possible social circles of Serbian society. Taking into consideration that a majority of the founders of the Belgrade Choral Society were German, along with a few Serbs, with Milan Milovuk at the head, then the situation is not surprising.

Above: National Theatre, Belgrade.

In Belgrade during this period there was a large number of foreigners—businessmen mainly from Austria. For their cultural and artistic needs, they brought in mostly German societies. For example, in 1844, the Muzikalno Drustvo Blagorodnog Gospodina od Hellenbah (The Music Society of the Noble Gentleman from Hellenbach) organized a grand musical concert to celebrate the opening of its new building on Elena Street in Belgrade. Its program reveals the musical taste of the day—Mozart, Rossini and other European composers of the period.

When Stevan Todorovic moved to Belgrade in May of 1857, he became a member of the Society and remarked that the choral pieces were *"mostly bourgeois songs"* or those of the European middle class. Smarting from the repressive Austro-Hungarian rule in his native Vojvodina, he continued, *"To me it was not pleasant that in a Serbian concert hall, in a Serbian society, German was sung. In agreement with the good Serb and poet, Jovo Ilic, we succeeded, at least, in having the texts translated into Serbian."* Emilian Josimovic and Ljuba Nenadovic also participated in these reform attempts.

Unfortunately, there was not much Serbian music available, so the Society continued with Serbian words sung to German melodies. Todorovic suggested they sing the choral arrangements of a young, Serbian composer, Kornelije Stankovic, whose pieces were marked by light and simple harmony. This idea was not accepted—as director Milovuk believed, *"Music has no nationality."* Therefore, all of Stevan Todorovic's attempts, between 1857 and 1863, to have the Belgrade Choral Society take a *"nationalistic turn"* were without success.

This tension continued until the appearance of Kornelije Stankovic in 1863, when the question of the direction of the Belgrade Choral Society was definitively solved. The by-laws of 1864 clearly state the Society's purpose to *"spread and support the development of music in the fatherland, the awakening of a love of music, keeping in view the nature of Slavic and Serbian music."* With those words, they expressed not only their goal but also the sphere of the Society's work. Therefore the work of Kornelije Stankovic and what it meant to the musical culture of Serbia is not difficult to understand, given the musical opportunities in Europe at that time.

In Europe there had developed several musical periods and styles through which reawakening musical form had developed to the fullest extent in terms of operatic, symphonic and chamber music compositions. The Classical Epoch was long passed, and, in place of it, musical Romanticism reigned. That was the time when the German Richard Wagner's musical dramas reached their climax and, to the greatest degree, awakened the musical soul of Europe. The Belgrade Choral Society with Kornelije Stankovic appeared at that very last moment of the Romantic reawakening.

Sadly, Kornelije's work with the Belgrade Choral Society did not last long. The creator of nationalism in Serbian music spent only slightly longer than a year with the Society. Already in March of 1864, his illness worsened. He went to Budapest for treatment and died there at Easter in 1865. The departure of Kornelije left the Society without the cohesive forces which had held all its members together. In spite of their personal differences of opinion, he held them together through the ideological foundations upon which he had based the Society's work.

The group around Milovuk, because of this same quarrel about Serbianism in music, totally withdrew from the Society. The new choir, which Stankovic had formed, was based on a group which separated itself from the old members. Stevan Todorovic was chosen as the first president of this new group, which kept the same name and the same rules. Thanks to him, the Belgrade Choral Society received a worthy representative for the new position of choir director in the Slovenian Davorin Jenko, the composer of the Slovenian and Serbian national anthems. He was suggested to the Society by Kornelije Stankovic. To Jenko belonged all the successes which the Belgrade Choral Society achieved and, in addition, credit for the production and reproduction of Serbian classical music—even if it was not always in the style and spirit of Kornelije Stankovic. During Jenko's tenure, the very Society, because of its work, was highly valued. This opinion was even more highly favorable, according to Jenko, because it came from the 90 year-old Stevan Todorovic—whom Jenko blamed for his exit from the Belgrade Choral Society.

The political friction in the country, and the wars of 1876-1878 were not without consequences in the work of the Belgrade Choral Society. The relations between the liberal and conservative wings of the political parties found their echoes in the relations of their members.

The younger members were liberal intellectuals who supported the United Serbian Youth (Ujedinjena Omladina Srpska), the opponents of Prince Michael Obrenovich. Opposite them was a smaller group of older conservative members, Prince Michael's supporters. That was inevitably carried over to the internal conflicts in the Society itself. Finding support among the concert public, the youth carried on a persistent struggle and finally succeeded in getting predominance in the Society.

Only in that can one understand the Society's participation in the United Serbian Youth conference in Novi Sad in 1866. The Society was the organizer of its next conference which was held in Belgrade in 1867. The clash of the youths with Prince Michael following the second conference led to the fall of the Society's leadership.

Clearly, in the Belgrade Choral Society there was always enough young strength from Serbia's progressive people whose cultural and artistic work of the 1870s rested on healthy political foundations. Its work led to wide national significance.

The consequences of the rocky relations among the Choral Society's membership reverberated in the life of the Society itself. In the apathy which took over after the fall of its officers in 1867, it did not progress. They sang old numbers and, at that, without feeling.

Around 1877, the Society was back to its own full life and became a strong artistic body. The Society strengthened its internal organizational structure and widened its scope by founding its own library and reading room, as well as a school, in 1876. This school was a remnant of the earlier preparatory choir school founded by Kornelije Stankovic. The members of this choir, by finishing courses, could be accepted for regular membership in the Society.

By founding a mixed choir in 1880, mainly to the credit of Stevan Sram, the Belgrade Choral Society was fulfilling the spirit of its rules by which every honorable person could become a member of the Society without regard to sex, religion or nationality. The democratic nature, political maturity, and progressive attitude of these rules made the Belgrade Choral Society of 1880, contemporary in the full meaning of the word.

In Belgrade more and more choirs were being heard—choirs born in the spirit of nationalism in music, until, in the development of political programs, each was pressured to develop and present greater and better known works of Serbian and other Slavic choir music.

Among its work were independent concerts arranged for benevolent purposes—for hospitals caring for the poor in 1865, for helping poor students in 1866, for the founding of the National Theatre in 1869, for the rebellion in Bosnia and Hercegovina in 1875, for a society founded to help the wounded Serbian rebels in Bosnia and Hercegovina in 1876, and for those Serbs who suffered in the war of 1877. At the beginning of 1879, the Belgrade Choral Society organized a private concert for the benefit of the family of the late, beloved poet Djura Jaksic. Arranged on a benevolent basis, these concerts had a special significance for the cultural and artistic work of this group and for the musical life of Belgrade and Serbia in the 1860s and 1870s. The Choral Society had exerted a great influence on musical life in general. That is shown by the appearance of a large number of new choirs formed just after the Belgrade Choral Society. In Belgrade itself there were three more, and inside Serbia six more were formed.

For its success in the period between Kornelije Stankovic and Josif Marinkovic, the Belgrade Choral Society must thank one of its presidents—Stevan Todorovic—artist, actor, concert singer, teacher, and organizer of everything with immediate ties to the cultural life of the city of Belgrade in his time. His work with the Choral Society distinguished itself by sincere and progressive artistic awakening, regardless of his close ties to conservative royal circles. He was also involved in selecting Stevan Mokranjac, from among the members of the Belgrade Choral Society, to study music abroad.

The Choral Society celebrated its 30th Anniversary in 1882. Stevan Todorovic triumphed at that time by getting the first Serb since Kornelije Stankovic to head the choir. He was Josif Marinkovic (1851-1931), who, with his work and ideas for vocal music, brought life and inspiration to the work of the Society. In the first thirty years, 1853-1883, the Belgrade Choral Society became the nucleus around which Serbian classical music developed. Under the guidance of able leaders and talented composers, the Society became a major cultural institution. By 1883, Kornelije Stankovic had died, and Davorin Jenko had left. A new leader emerged: Josif Marinkovic.

His compositions played on the characteristic folk music. From these sources came his kolos and patriotic songs, which—in the Romantic period of the 1880s—warmed audiences and fostered pride in Serbian culture. Even today, some of his works, like *Narodni zbor*, (National Gathering) have freshness, beauty and relevance. Marinkovic remained with the Belgrade Choral Society a short time, between 1881 and 1887, but left behind a visible trace, a large number of prepared concert programs which were imprinted with the indelible mark of his compositions—*Kola, Narodni zbor, Jadna majka*, and others. The tone of the musical programs, for the first time since Kornelije Stankovic were of a pure national character.

Marinkovic's successor, Stevan Mokranjac, appeared on the Serbian music scene as choir director at the most opportune moment—just when Serbian urban society was mature. The grand successes which the Society enjoyed during the period of his leadership, from 1887 to 1914, are attributed to his remarkable ability both as a composer and choir director. As a stipendist of the Belgrade Choral Society, and later of the Serbian national leaders, Mokranjac between 1879 and 1887 studied music in Munich, Rome and Leipzig. It was Society President Stevan Todorovic who borrowed money for him many times both from the Belgrade Choral Society and outside the organization. The Belgrade metropolitan of the Serbian Orthodox Church also helped.

Mokranjac, the creator of *Rukovet*, was a composer with a natural sensitivity for folk melody and for both spiritual and secular music. He was the originator of our Serbian musical taste and the first Serbian composer of the Realist movement. He remained for many long years the central figure in the musical life of Serbia.

Working at the Belgrade Choral Society for a quarter of a century, he assumed a dominant position as the composer, director, music teacher, and organizer. With his remarkable energy, he elevated music production and reproduction in Belgrade to a new level such as before him only Davorin Jenko or Josif Marinkovic had achieved. As the creator, he was singularly active and singularly successful in both secular and religious music. In these years, the Choral Society greatly enlarged the sphere of its influence by appearing outside Belgrade. Smederevo was the first city beyond Belgrade in which its missionary word was heard in 1883. Sremska Mitrovica was the first Serbian city of the Vojvodina to hear the apostolic Serbian nationalist music in 1891.

After the Smederevo performance, their tour covered most of Serbia. There is not one large city in Serbia in which the Belgrade Choral Society did not perform, achieving a direct influence on the development of concert music for the entire Serbian music world.

What resulted from the Society members' visits to cities with Serbian inhabitants in Austria is undisputed—they left a deep imprint on the cultural and political consciousness of the Serbs living there. In this respect, their visit to Dubrovnik and Kotor in 1893 had the same effect. The Belgrade Choral Society arrived in Dubrovnik to perform at the dedication of a monument to the revered Dubrovnik poet Ivan Gundulic (1589-1638). This visit triggered a nationalistic demonstration by the local Serbs and Austrian authorities intervened, fearing the unification of the Serbs of Dubrovnik with the Serbs of Serbia.

One of its most memorable successes abroad was the 1894 concert in Budapest. The Hungarian critic Edjetertes classified the Belgrade Choral Society with the famous and revered Slavic Choir. In fact, he gave the Belgrade Choral Society even higher marks because its *"choir has a bass who surpasses even the famous Slavic bass."* Another Hungarian critic, Pester Loyd, called Mokranjac an outstandingly artistic choir director *"sensitive and of extremely good taste."* As for the Belgrade Choral Society, he said they are on *"such an elevated artistic height that they do not have to fear comparison to any other choir in Europe."*

Like the other concerts, this visit of Serbs to the Austro-Hungarian Monarchy had *"yet another ramification"* in regard to the harsh Hungarian political rule and its poor relations with Serbs within the Dual Monarchy.

Following the concert, the Serbs of Budapest went out and stood on the road nearest Serbia. There they questioned the authorities as to why there was a barrier between Serbs on each side of the Danube and Sava rivers. According to the Serbs in the Austro-Hungarian Monarchy, the barriers were erected simply to prevent the Serbs of Serbia from coming to the Monarchy, and, in turn, to make it necessary for Serbs in Hungary to get Hungarian permission to make visits to their brother Serbs. The Belgrade Choral Society saw the problem as a challenge. After it performed in Budapest to rave reviews, there was not a village where Serbs lived in Hungary in which the Belgrade Choral Society could not perform. Even the Dual Monarchy did not stop them..

The success in Budapest only served to reaffirm their earlier brilliant successes at Skoplje, Salonika, and Vranje, but after Budapest, the Society's stature grew even more with the public and with other choral groups of Belgrade. The well-known and strong choral society, Davorja, merged with the Belgrade Choral Society on February 22, 1895. They performed in the Turkish Empire at Sofia, Plovdiv, and Istanbul in 1895; in Imperial Russia at St. Petersburg, Novgorod, Moscow, and Kiev in 1896; and in Germany and Austria at Berlin, Dresden, and Leipzig in 1899.

Without a doubt, these represented the high point of the Belgrade Choral Society's artistic achievement in the decades since its founding in 1853. This showed that even the most discerning of European critics, especially the Russians and the Germans, agreed on the Society's outstanding technical achievements, their grand artistic ability, and the cultural value of Serbian music. Their fame had spread not only throughout Serbia and Belgrade, but also abroad.

Like Davorja had following Budapest, the ecclesiastical choir society Kornelije Stankovic merged with the Belgrade Choral Society on October 14, 1896, after the concerts in Russia. At that time the

Society divided into two branches—one for secular music and the other, under the name of Kornelije Stankovic, for liturgical music. With this merger, the Belgrade Choral Society agreed to perform at Belgrade's Serbian Orthodox Cathedral, and, for this work, to accept regular payments from both the Church Governing Board and the Council of Bishops. The successes of the Belgrade Choral Society came at the right time, as Austrian agents throughout Serbia circulated vicious rumors through the Serbian population. As a result of the divisions created and the court scandals of the last Obrenovich king, in 1903 there was a palace coup, and King Alexander and Queen Draga were assassinated. As a result, Serbia was vilified in the international press throughout Europe and in America. The European powers re-assessed their feelings and responsibilities toward this little nation of Serbia which, by its own effort, both economic and cultural, and was showing signs of success.

In all its work, the Belgrade Society proudly represented Serbia and had won a fine reception into the cultural community of nations. There was great proof Serbia's musical culture was being carried forth by the Belgrade Choral Society with Mokranjac at the head.

The collected programs and articles written at that time reveal that the Belgrade Choral Society was a strong and leading body capable of solving the complex problems of vocalization found in choral arrangements like the first eight-song collections of melodies from the Adriatic regions of Primorje by Stevan Mokranjac; the Johannes Brahms' choruses; and the music of Varlamov, Rimsky-Korsakov, Dimitri Bortnjanski, Maliskon, Franz Schubert, Franz Joseph Haydn, Josif Marinkovic, Topalovic, Davorin Jenko and others.

Without a doubt, the founding of its Serbian School of Music in 1899, the first school of its kind in Serbia, was a remarkable event in the cultural history of the country, equal only to the founding of the Belgrade Choral Society itself in 1853. The role the Society played in the creation of Serbian vocal music and choral reproductions is equivalent to the role its music school played in the creation of Serbian instrumental music and its reproduction and dissemination.

Among its many students who gained a basic knowledge of music methodology and artistry, we find names that bring honor to Serbian classical music—Miloje Milojevic, Kosta Manojlovic, and others. In this period, the Choral Society arranged concerts for helping various other groups, institutions, or individuals: the student group Pobratimstvo, a humanitarian fund for the war of 1885, celebrations of the Vuk Stefanovic Karadzic centennial in 1888, and the 500th Anniversary of the Battle of Kosovo in 1889. From the receipts of the 1889 concert at Kragujevac, they gave a donation to the Kosovo memorial fund.

The Society participated in a celebration honoring Simo Milutinovic, the teacher of the Montenegrin Prince-Bishop Petar Petrovic Njegos. In other words, the Society appeared every place it was necessary to show artistic, national, cultural, political, and social consciousness—and everywhere with success. Among these, the traditional New Year's Eve concerts stand out and it is possible they had been held since the Society's founding. The Society's patron saint, St. Vasilije, was celebrated for the first time in 1889 in addition to the religious concerts of Lent and Easter. At these, Mokranjac's compositions were met with unusually great success.

Credit must also be given the Society's president Djoko Stanojevic. During his tenure between 1882 and 1900, he showed a broad view and had courage akin to Stevan Todorovic before him. To Stanojevic, goes the credit for the fact that the Belgrade Choral Society carried forward its cultural duty inside Serbia and, as opportunities arose, initiated programs abroad.

> *And we, too, from the far-away north, draw near and thrill like every Serb to whom the Serbian songs are dear and beloved, and we are deeply thankful to those people who, in the course of the past half century, have taken out into the world the melodious and wonderful Serbian songs which, even in the darkest and most difficult days of oppression, preserved the Serbian name and gave it strength and life.*

Celebrating their 50th Anniversary in May, 1903, the Belgrade Choral Society performed works of everyone who worked in the field of Serbian music, giving the concert a grand historic significance. The very title, The *History of Serbian Songs in Concert*, reveals their goal. Just how powerfully the 50th Anniversary influenced the musical and national consciousness of Serbs, we can conclude from the reverberations both in and outside Serbia.

In that sense, the influence its music had on students is well known, for they, in every sense, had the greatest understanding of the work and goals of the Belgrade Choral Society, taking part themselves in every one of its efforts.

The letter from the Serbian students at St. Petersburg, Russia, characterizes the relationship that the Serbian youth had always enjoyed with the Belgrade Choral Society:

After the anniversary celebration, the Society brought to life one of its own dreams: the creation of the Serbian Choral Federation in which all the Serbian choral societies became members. With that, the musical culture of Serbia was finally organized. The Belgrade Choral Society thrilled at the new prospect. The selection of the strict constitutional leadership of Peter I Karadjordjevic as the King of Serbia in 1903 signalled the opening of freer expression of popular opinion. The results were the birth of reciprocal ties between Serbs, Croatians, and Slovenians built through official, cultural and artistic conferences.

Austria, even at this time, did not look kindly at the affinity between the Yugoslav peoples. The Tariff War of 1906-1911 and the Annexation of Bosnia-Hercegovina in 1908 were only preparatory phases in the Austrian politics of interference with Yugoslav unity. The Young Turks' Rebellion of 1908 and the Balkan Union of Serbia, Montenegro, Bulgaria and Greece in reaction to it, the Serbo-Bulgarian War of 1913, and the First World War of 1914-1918 completely filled the years of the first quarter of the 20th century. In light of the previous glorious era, war and crisis predominated and Belgrade was destroyed and occupied during the First World War. If we add to that the serious illness of Stevan Mokranjac in 1900 and again in 1911, and then the lower level of leadership following that, the image of a cultural giant being dismantled step by step emerges. In 1911, the Serbian School of Music separated from the Society. For this period there is little to say.

After World War I, in the new conditions offered by the unification of Serbs, Croats and Slovenes, the Choral Society immediately began work for the successful organization of the musical life in Belgrade and Serbia. The credit for this goes mainly to Kosta Manojlovic and his choir direction between 1919 and 1931. His work is characterized by sincere integrated Yugoslavism.

In June of 1925, the selected concert piece was *Missa papae Marcelli,* and some considered it an attack on Serbian Orthodoxy. The Yugoslav Concert in April of 1926 even better illustrates Manojlovic as a Yugoslav. At that concert, along with modern works of Serbian, Croatian, and Slovenian composers he selected two chorals by the Bulgarian composer Dobri Hristov, *Petra, Petruvljanka* and *Slana padna Gane*. Because of this, the concert was booed by a group of extreme elements, who, in honor of Serbian casualties in the First World War, blamed all the Bulgarian politicians who had led Bulgaria to the Axis Powers opposing Serbia.

Of the outstanding performances in the period, the English Madrigal Concert and the Yugoslav Concert, both in 1929, the second was given in celebration of the Society's 75th Anniversary. Manojlovic's goal was to once again raise the Society to the level it enjoyed between 1894 and 1903, and he was successful in a measure that surpassed all expectation. The chorus became the leading body in style of concert programs.

At the end of the last century and, to a great degree, at the beginning of this, there appeared in Serbia musical professionalism—and, with that, the Society of Serbian Musicians was founded in 1907 with Mokranjac at its head. Even if the idea for the founding belongs to Boza Joksimovic, there is no doubt that the Belgrade Choral Society participated in its founding. Mokranjac himself was a member of the committee for the writing of its by-laws, and right beside him, from the Belgrade Choral Society, was Petar Krstic. In this same way, the Society took part in the founding of the South Slavic Choral Society in 1924 and of the First Yugoslav Musical Exhibition in 1926—about which it can be said, in truth, that they were Manojlovic's projects. He also founded the Music Museum in 1927, at his own expense, as the first of its kind in Serbia. It was his institution. Given its new Yugoslav nature, the Belgrade Choral Society chose two Croatians as presidents: Dr. Victor Novak in 1925, a university professor and former president of the Croatian Choral Society Lisinski from Zagreb, and Dr. Ivan Ribar, past president of the Yugoslav National Assembly.

After 1929, the Society's entered the fourth quarter of its first hundred years. It continued to be the leader in the musical life of Belgrade and Serbia. Even so, its influence was no longer felt to the great extent that it had been before the turn of the century. In Novi Sad, Subotica, Vukovar, Sombor, Sarajevo, Mostar and the other larger cities in Yugoslavia, there were strong Serbian choral societies capable of rendering the most complex vocal arrangements and claiming for themselves the role of musical leader for their local regions.

Following the Society's failure at the Jamboree of 1929 and the crisis of 1930-1931, Manojlovic resigned as director and a small number of dissatisfied members joined him. In 1932, the Society regained its lost position. joined him. In 1932, the Society regained its lost position. The more it broadened to unimagined new heights, the more it succeeded. Around 1937, the Society reached the very highest level of its development. In that year, together with its artistic leader Predrag Milosevic, it stood at the very top of all European a cappella choral groups. Milosevic had joined the Society in 1932. Second only to Mokranjac, who in the earlier period of Romanticism composed the greatest artistic range and achieved the greatest success of the Society, Milosevic's selection of choral material represented the greatest range of artistic content the Belgrade Choral Society ever performed. The results were astounding. Its greatest success in the history of the Society and its restoration to health was signalled by the presentation of Handel's *Messiah* on April 8, 1937, which represented the most outstanding work of classical instrumental literature and demanded a highly developed technical and artistic skill.

Black war clouds were already visible in Europe. We knew they would pass over to our land. The First Belgrade Choral Society knew that too, because it had always participated and shared all the important events of its homeland—it could feel national danger. With the occupation of World War II, the Belgrade Choral Society found itself literally on the street. The Germans, immediately upon entering Belgrade, took over the primary school at the Serbian Orthodox Cathedral in which the Society had been quartered since 1921. The Society headquarters, its archives, library, and all other Belgrade Choral Society materials were thrown on the street, too. Suddenly gone was the Society's notes, its important documents, and old, priceless music publications by the early Serbian composers, without which today we can hardly imagine going on. There was information about the musical and cultural history of the Serbs on *both sides* of the Sava and Danube rivers. It was all suddenly gone.

Thanks to the Serbian Orthodox Cathedral, space was made available for what archives survived. Choir rehearsals began to be held at the church offices. That is how the Cathedral in Belgrade got the Belgrade Choral Society to participate in the Sunday and holiday religious services.

One thing is certain; as long as it exists, it will strive to be what it was. It has shown the will to survive, to create, and that is enough to affirm that it will find itself in the future. For the Belgrade Choral Society, this first period of cultural history was the very foundation of all musical life from which flowed for one hundred years everything that Serbs have today in the area of modern classical music. This important period gave rise to composers, choir directors, music teachers, opera singers, and, above all, organizations for our musical life—it will not be difficult for the Belgrade Choral Society to find the high road in the second century of its full and rich life.

The 1853 Board of The Belgrade Choral Society:

President—Stevan Todorovic
J. Marinkovic, L. Kapelan, J. Petrovic,
M. Stanojevic, N. D'Andrea,
R. Nikolic, E. Derok, K. Petrovic,
J. Radulovic, D. D'Andrea.

The Belgrade Choral Society article was supplied by the Serb National Federation. This is an edited version of the original twelve-page article published in Belgrade in 1953.

# VLAJKO

### the man, his music and the organization he founded

by Paul S. Bielich and Paul S. Papich

Vladimir M. Lugonja is one of the most admired Serbs in America. Known to his friends affectionately as *"Vlajko,"* he was the founder of the Serbian Singing Federation of America (U.S.A. and Canada). That unquestionably qualified him as one of the greatest youth leaders of all time. The organization he began 60 years ago is today among the most successful and vital forces in American Serb life. Serbian music and Serbian Orthodox Church choirs in America owe their very existence to this man of exceptional foresight.

Vlajko Lugonja was the first among us to understand the urgent need for a national organization which could serve as a pivotal force to deter the demise of Serbian music, both popular and religious. In 1931, when the continent was reeling from the financial devastation caused by the stock market crash, Lugonja decided it was time for Serbian youth in America to—of all things—start *singing!* As incongruous as it may seem for a man to invest his life's energy in the simple act of singing at a time when the world was rocked by economic disaster, it is no less incongruous that the very man to do so came from the humblest of beginnings and rose to head a large international organization whose goals and principles are truly lofty ideals.

Vladimir M. Lugonja was born on February 9, 1898, in Chemerno, one of the smallest villages in Herzegovina, Yugoslavia.

Vlajko attended public school in Gacko for two years, the only formal Serbian education he was lucky enough to receive before immigrating to the United States at the age of 9. With his father, a former merchant and political refugee, and his sister, Radojka, Vlajko came to Chicago, Illinois, on April 12, 1907. There they lived with Vlajko's uncle, Acim Lugonja, who was a very active member of the early Chicago Serbian community. Another sister, Draginja, had stayed behind in Europe with her grandmother.

A few years after his arrival, Vlajko played the *biserica tambura* with a group of young men called *"Srbadija."* The orchestra was not interested in material wealth; they only played for the love of Serbian music and donated any money received to the Church. In this early unselfish style, the pattern for Vlajko's later efforts is evident. On behalf of a crusade to preserve the culture of his people, Vlajko later submerged his own personal identity.

At the age of 15 he became the youngest member of the Branko Radicevich Choir in Chicago. He was recruited by Mr. Stevo Bogdanovich when there was a shortage of tenors—but because of his high lyric tenor voice which did not blend with the rest, there was some question as to whether Director Arno Mario Hess would allow him to continue. Continue he did until he moved to Detroit—where his sister, Radojka had moved when she married Chris Petrouleas, a restaurant owner. Later his father left Chicago for Detroit, and Vlajko missed his family. So he, too, was in Detroit living with his sister and brother-in-law.

Missing his early experiences in Chicago with the Branko Radicevich Choir, Vlajko took decisive action—as he did many times in his long life—and rallied his new male friends organizing Detroit's first choir, the Philip Visnich Choir. Because of a lack of music and poor communication with other groups, the Philip Visnich Choir was short-lived. Not to be defeated, in 1930 Vlajko organized the choir which continues to this very day, the Ravanica.

Experience taught Vlajko Lugonja no choir can exist long by itself. Armed with this insight, he persisted in his efforts toward a national organization. He wrote a series of 12 articles in *The American Srbobran* during 1930 and 1931 which awakened so much interest in his Serbian brothers and sisters that they quickly responded to his ideas with wholehearted support. Encouraged by this response, he called a conference of *"lovers of Serbian music"* in March of 1931 at the Christopher House. In October of the same year, the Serbian Singing Federation was formally organized as a completely independent non-profit organization. Petar Sekulovich, Karl Malden's father, was elected as the first president. At that time there were only 5 participating choirs.

Vlajko wrote, *"Brighten up your community and help make the new year (1932) happy with our own songs and music!"* For the first 5 years the headquarters were in Highland Park, Michigan. At the first convention Lugonja was elected executive secretary, a position he held for over 30 years. The first choral festival was held in Akron, Ohio on Memorial Day weekend, 1936, with 16 member choirs participating. In his work, Vlajko Lugonja was indefatigable. Practically every choir was personally brought in by him. To accomplish his goals, Lugonja drew upon tremendous energy reserves not available to most men. He made personal sacrifices travelling and organizing new choirs. The success of the federation can be attributed to Vlajko's foresight in seeing the need for such a group and to his perseverance in creating interest among the original 5 choirs. This movement perhaps more than any other brought the young Serbian Americans closer to each other, to their Eastern Orthodox Church and to their Serbian culture. The Depression years were difficult for everyone, and economic survival was of major concern. For a brief period Vlajko worked as a publicity consultant for Mihajlo Duchich's Cloverleaf Dairy in Gary, Indiana. In 1938 he moved to New York City for a job at the Consulate of the Royal Yugoslav Government. The contacts he made there helped him collect Serbian music in order to preserve it on the North American continent.

In 1937 he went on a tour of Yugoslavia with a group of American Serbs sponsored by the Serb National Federation. While there, he met many composers and the families of the greats of the past. As a result, a wealth of music was collected. Because of his efforts, today's Serbian Singing Federation has the single richest collection of Serbian choral music in the world. Many of the compositions cannot even be found in Yugoslavia today, as the originals were destroyed in the German attacks on Belgrade in 1941.

By travelling throughout the United States and Canada, Vlajko personally organized many choirs and, by the beginning of World War II, had increased the membership of the federation to 30. During the war years,

*Above:* The first SSF Festival in 1936 with sixteen choirs performing the finale.
Vlajko Lugonja seen center front. Photo courtesy of The Serbian Singing Federation.

there were no festivals; only one convention was held. His considerable energy was put into working as a press correspondent for the *Srpska Narodna Odbrana* (Serbian National Defense) and coordinating the shipment of literally thousands of parcels of food and clothing to Serbian war refugees. Immediately after the war, Vlajko renewed his efforts on behalf of the SSF—and the membership continued to increase. He was provided his rent and a small monthly promotional expense by the SSF.

Vlajko Lugonja and Paul Bielich.
Photo courtesy of the SSF.

Thirty-one years after his work had begun, in 1962, Vladimir M. Lugonja relinquished his position as executive secretary in order to retire. The convention bestowed upon him the title of *"honorary executive secretary"* by acclamation. He continued to work for his beloved federation in public relations, music research and publishing.

In September of 1977, Vladimir M. Lugonja died. He was buried from Detroit's Ravanica Serbian Orthodox Church. His remains are now at St. Sava Serbian Orthodox Monastery Cemetery, Libertyville, Illinois. In his 80 years, Vlajko had dedicated himself to the creation and preservation of the Serbian Singing Federation. To this day, his influence is felt through the many member choirs who continue to benefit from the life's work of this truly great man.

## Serbian Singing Federation

Before the turn of the century Serbs were flocking to this continent to seek a better life. As early as 1906 the first Serbian choir in North America was founded. The *S.S.S. Branko Radichevich Choir* of Chicago exists today and can be credited for the federations and beneficial associations that followed, including the Serbian Orthodox Diocese of North America.

The 5 charter member choirs of the SSF are the Branko Radichevich Choir of Chicago, Sloboda of Chicago, Karageorge of Gary, Ravanica of Detroit and Vojvoda Putnick of Youngstown.

New choirs were organized and old ones reactivated following a long series of articles in *The American Srbobran*—a national choral festival was called for May, 1936 on Memorial Day weekend in Akron, Ohio and 16 choirs responded to this first festival. Local papers carried headlines that *"5,000 Come Here For Singing Convention."* More than a 1,000 were from member choirs—they overwhelmed the local hotels to such a degree that some people needed to be housed in the police station and others in a local hospital.

In the early years the SSF member choirs were divided into 2 divisions—east and west—and generally into 3 categories: mixed, male, and female. Festivals were held every 2 years and were of a competitive nature. Eliminations were held in both the western and eastern divisions, culminating in the final contest.

Three of the most qualified, paid, professional judges in the hosting city were contracted to choose the best singing choir using an arithmetical rating system. One of the judges was Serbian or of some other Slavic descent, acting as a guide on proper diction, style and interpretation, while the other 2 handled the more technical aspects of composition.

It was an exciting era for choirs and audiences who reaped the benefit of the sounds of the finest in Serbian choral compositions. The competitive festivals kept the choirs up at the top of their strength, numerically and musically, inspired them to attend rehearsals, cooperate with plans for the future and consider their singing more seriously. They brought out the best efforts on the part of the directors, some of whom needed the little stimulant that only a competitive festival can bring forth.

It was that something *"extra"* which old timers will remember from past festivals. From the point of audience appeal, the competitive festivals drew much more because of the interest people naturally have in a contest between young groups for excellence in their chosen field of musical art.

Searching for appropriate awards to be made to contest winners, SSF secretary, the late V. M. Lugonja, prevailed upon Mrs. Barbara Pupin Smith to donate a silver cup in memory of her father, inventor Mihajlo Pupin—who was a lover of choral singing and an admirer of the SSF movement. The first prize winner gained possession of the coveted Michael Pupin Memorial Cup, a masterpiece of handwrought English sterling silver valued at $1,500. The male choirs competed for the Nikola Perazich Cup and the women's choral groups for a cup donated by the Serbian Women's Organizations.

The *"Pupin Cup"* quickly became the envied symbol that all choirs strived to obtain. Professor Alexander Savine, the internationally famous composer and choral director, whose able and patient tutoring of the younger generation of singers of Branko Radichevich, brought his group to the foreground of Chicagoland singing choirs that won them the highest honors, winning the SSF National Championship both at the 1936 and the 1938 festivals.

In the third festival, after being proclaimed the western winner, their disappointment was keenly felt by the singers and the entire community when—following an arithmetical error by one of the judges—the Gary Karageorge Choir was selected to represent the west in the finals. It was Cleveland's *Njegosh Choir* that won the National Championship in 1940 and the right to the Pupin Cup for a year.

The SSF wisely discontinued competitive festivals because many singers went away disappointed. It was decided to *"sing for the glory of God and the honor of our people,"* believing that if a choir of 30-40 singers was able to make a 300-400 mile trip that was reward enough.

The famed Pupin Cup can be seen at SSF headquarters in Madison Heights, Michigan, where singers can recall and view an archive of the *"silver era"* of SSF singing.

During the Second World War, choral activities were greatly reduced. Many choirs became temporarily inactive and the membership of the SSF fell from nearly 30 to only 11. During the war years, there were no festivals and only one convention. Singers assisted SSF secretary, Vlajko Lugonja, in the shipment of thousands of parcels of clothes and food to war refugees. After the war, the SSF regained its former membership.

In 1948, the SSF sponsored its first post-war festival in Pittsburgh, which was a great success. The festival drew 19 participating choirs and thousands of Serbs from throughout the nation. Hosts for the occasion were the 7 Serbian choirs of the Pittsburgh area—Aliquippa, Clairton, Pittsburgh, McKeesport, Duquesne Midland, Wilmerding and Youngwood.

The festival was recorded by the United States State Department and 8 songs were selected for broadcasting over Voice of America and the BBC to Yugoslavia and other countries behind the Iron Curtain.

One of the greatest honors that can come to a Serbian artists is to be chosen to sing to and for the SSF singers, a most coveted engagement—a veritable command performance—of which any singer should be proud. The SSF over the years has been blessed with the appearances of many fine soloists including: Mitar Bulatovich, Danica Chirich, Vinka Ellesin, Militza Kosanchich, Milutin Lazich, Mija Novich, Sophia Topalsky Papich, Rasha Radenkovich, Uros Seferovich, Milan Timotich, Helen Tomich, Angelina Vlajkovich, and Paul Zelich (see pgs. 62-63).

Sloboda, 1927—the first Serbian choir in America.
Photo courtesy of Mitzi Alexich.

The tradition of choir concerts has continued to remain a strength of the SSF. Choirs annually sponsor a concert inviting another distant SSF member choir to be their weekend guests. It is here that Serbian hospitality, music, and song are united to establish lifelong friendships among singers. Choirs anticipate with great enthusiasm the invitation to be the guests of another member choir.

Most important to the success of any choir is its director. Recognizing the fact that the directors of all member choirs are important, a history of the SSF would not be complete without naming those who have achieved and contributed to the national SSF namely: V. Rev. Milan Markovina, Nada Milosevich, Adam Popovich, George Milan Radakovich, Nikola Resanovic and Slobodan Zelich. The SSF also owes a great debt of gratitude to †Peter Bila, †Boris Dobrovolsky, †V. Rev. Dr. Milan G. Popovich, †Alexander Savine and †V. Rev. Sava Vujov.

America's Bicentennial did not go by unnoticed, as choirs from coast to coast participated in Bicentennial concerts. Of notable accomplishment in the Midwest was the Milwaukee SSS Stevan Sijacki and South Chicago SSS Sloboda—who combined in a musical extravaganza to perform Ljubomir Bosnjakovich's cantata *Albanksa golgota,* among other compositions. The Milwaukee Symphony Orchestra and Chicago Civic Orchestra cooperated in providing orchestral accompaniment to the 2 concert programs. The Petar Krstich Choir of Steubenville, Ohio, also celebrated the Bicentennial with a performance of the *Albanska golgota.*

The SSF returned to the city of Akron, Ohio for the Bicentennial Festival which drew a record number of choirs and spectators. The Stevan Hristich Choir of Phoenix made the trip to Akron and accepted the SSF's invitation to be the honored church choir for the festival—the first Western choir to appear at an SSF festival.
Saturday's concert was held in the new and modern St. Archangel Michael Serbian Hall, while Sunday's concert was held in the Performing Arts Building of the University of Akron. Mrs. Sophia Papich, festival guest soloist, entertained at the Sunday performance in her special style that led her to being acclaimed among the best of Serbian soloists. The Petar Krstich Serbian Choir of Steubenville, Ohio sang Bosnjakovich's *Albanska Golgota.*

As the nation paid tribute to its founding fathers, the Serbian Singing Federation likewise honored its founder, Vlajko Lugonja. A testimonial sponsored by the S.S.S. Ravanica was held at the Hillcrest Country Club in suburban Detroit, where singers gathered from many choirs and colonies to pay tribute to their founder. Special guest/speakers included: Rt. Rev. Dr. Bishop Firmilian, toastmaster, Bill Salatich, SSF vice president, Kosta Papich, SSF executive secretary, Paul S. Bielich, SNF president, Robert Rade Stone.

While the SSF cooperates with the Serbian Church on a national basis and all Serbian churches on a local level, the SSF is a separate, non-profit organization. Its purpose is to organize and coordinate the efforts of member choirs through festivals, choral workshops, conventions, recordings and scholarship fundraising. The primary responsibility of each member choir is to sing responses to the Divine Liturgy every Sunday in their local churches. Through its choirs, the SSF seeks to perpetuate among Americans and Canadians of Serbian descent the priceless cultural heritage of their Church and secular music.

Every effort is made to incorporate more religious education into the Federation. The first concrete attempt has been at the national conventions, where a noted religious educator or other informed person on Serbianism and Orthodoxy is given the keynote spot.

The greatest wealth of the Serbian Singing Federation is in its Library, comprising the works of 96 Serbian composers with thousands of musical scores. It has been said that the Federation Library is more complete than any Serbian music collection in the world.

*Left:* Vlajko Lugonja arriving at the festival by train in Akron in 1936, shown with the Maksimovich Brothers —Jovan, Branko, Ivan and Milan Maksimovich. Photo courtesy of Branko Maksimovich.

The publishing of Serbian choral compositions is an important aspect of the Serbian Singing Federation. Close to 200 compositions have been published which are furnished free of charge to member choirs. A Music Publishing Committee guides the publications of new musical scores. Publication costs are often defrayed by donations from individuals and/or organizations who contribute toward the publication of a musical composition. Although many individuals have lent assistance in the necessary pre-publication tasks, Dragie Cucujlevich Zuzuly of Chicago and V. Rev. Milan Markovina of Milwaukee deserve special recognition and tribute.

The Serbian Singing Federation is eternally grateful to Dragie Cucujlevich Zuzuly, son of SSF vice president, the late Bozo Cucujlevich, for providing the SSF in 1950 with a composite book of responses to the Divine Liturgy. This much needed Liturgy was deemed easy enough for the average choir, yet contained some compositions for the more advanced choirs who wish to change their responses from time to time. Dragie embarked upon a venture—a labor of love—which took much of his spare time for nearly 2 years to complete.

He made the selections, copied all the notes and texts and crowded as much into the 64 pages as the space permitted. Affectionately referred to as the *green book* by singers, this composite Liturgy is still in use and demanded by many choirs today and necessitated a reprinting in recent years. The greatest stride forward for the SSF during the last decade was the purchase of a permanent Headquarters and Library in Madison Heights, Michigan, a suburb of Detroit. In the short period of 2 years the SSF collected the necessary funds needed to pay off the mortgage, and under the

*Above Left:* St. Steven's Serbian Orthodox Cathedral Choir of Alhambra, California (1960). Photo courtesy of Betty Kovacevich. *Above Right:* George Milan Radakovich, director of St. Steven's Choir for 44 years. Photo courtesy of St. Steven's Cathedral Choir. *Bottom left:* Sloboda performing on stage at St. Steven's Cathedral in 1956. *Bottom Right:* Adam Popovich, director of the Serbian Singing Society Sloboda for 60 years. He retired in 1997. Photos courtesy of Mitzi Alexich.

presidency of Dr. Richard Goich the Headquarters building was paid off. A gala mortgage burning banquet celebrated this great accomplishment.

An ongoing fund-raising campaign solicits funds for the purpose of adding to the Library everything available—published, copied or photocopied in Serbian music in the last century. Choral music, books on history, drama, poetry and other cultural subjects for the enjoyment, preservation and perpetuation of our Serbian heritage and song in all its various forms will be available for all who can make use of it, in addition to our member choirs and the fast emerging tamburitza and kolo groups throughout the United States and Canada.
The Serbian Singing Federation Headquarters and Library located in Madison Heights, Michigan and is administered by SSF executive secretary, Paul S. Bielich. Visitors to the Detroit area are encouraged and welcomed to stop in and visit.

The sacrifices of many have collectively brought about the birth of the Serbian Singing Federation and its growth and prosperity over the past 65 years. Our common interest to uphold and to keep alive, in America and Canada, the beautiful and nostalgic Serbian songs is a bond of fraternal kinship which we cherish. Our common endeavor is to leave a heritage of songs to the future generations. Our aim is that those who take up where we leave off find the spiritual inspirations and musical happiness that we have with our member choirs.

*Pesma nas je odrzala, njozi hvala.*

The Vlajko article was provided by the Serbian Singing Federation.

*Below:* Very Rev. Dr. Milan Popovich, priest, musician, educator, shown with the Isidor Bajich Choir of Akron, Ohio, in 1932. While Sloboda was the first Serbian choir in America, in 1927, the Bajich Choir was the first Serbian Orthodox Church choir in the United States. *Shown above are:* Dorothy Adamov, Mike Adamov, Sally Ardeljan, Olga Chokovan, Mitzie Chirich, Dan Davidovac, Elizabeth Davidov, Dorothy Dubotin, Mike Evkovich, Sam Gable, Rose Gerich, Pearl Gichanov, Edythe Hadnadjev, Olga Hadnadjev, Geraldine Kizmik, Olga Kizmik, Nick Koval, Dorothy Lekich, Smilja Lonchar, Rose Marko, Sam Maximovich, Serge Migdal, Geraldine Millich, Perry Millich, Evelyn Miskovich, Millie Nester, Josephine Okljesha, Alexander Pavlov, Louise Penjin, Stanley Plackovich, Paul Povich, Rudy Pozunitz, Ann Rudich, Irene Shatrich, Bosko Simich, Steve Srdanov, Kay Vasich, Kathryn Velimirovich, Millee Velimirovich, Mary Yovanovich, Alexander Vuchich and George Zlichich. Photo courtesy of the Serb National Federation.

# Tsar Lazar Male Choir of Pittsburgh
*The newest member of the Serbian Singing Federation*

Tsar Lazar is a select male choir comprised of men from 6 Serbian Orthodox parishes in Pennsylvania and Ohio, supplemented by several singers from Russian, Carpatho-Russian and Ukrainian parishes. The choir was founded in the Spring of 1991 by singers from several member choirs of the Serbian Singing Federation. The choir is directed by Mark Doncic.

Tsar Lazar is committed to the preservation and perpetuation of Serbian Orthodox liturgical and choral music, as well as the rich repertoire of Serbian folk music. It seeks to project the virtues of this extensive cultural heritage to audiences in and beyond the Serbian communities in America and Canada.

The Tsar Lazar Male Choir has performed to acclaim at concerts in Chicago, Illinois, Los Angeles, Toronto and Windsor, Ontario.

In 1998, Tsar Lazar became an Associate Member choir of the Serbian Singing Federation (SSF). The choir has 6 singers who have performed in the SSF choirs of their home parishes for more than 50 years, and takes pride in having 2 former Presidents of the Serbian Singing Federation in its ranks, as well as the current president of the Serb National Federation, George Martich.

Tsar Lazar's first recording, *"Soul of Tsar Lazar,"* is comprised of 18 sacred Orthodox hymns. In the Fall of 1997, the recording was selected by WQED-FM, Pittsburgh's listener-supported classical station, as a special gift for contributors during the station's annual fund raising drive.

Mark Doncic, Director

Tsar Lazar Director Mark Doncic, 38, is a native of Toronto, Canada, where he first began directing the St. Sava Serbian Orthodox Church choir at the age of 18. Before beginning his directing career, Mark studied piano for a decade with Dr. John Younger, a renowned Canadian musician who developed the musical curriculum for that nation's Royal Conservatory. While still residing in Toronto, Mr. Doncic, an accomplished tenor, sang with the Christ The Savior Russian Orthodox Cathedral Choir. Upon taking a position in London, Ontario, Mr. Doncic became the founding director of the St. Sava Serbian Orthodox Church choir in that community. There he also sang with the Mendelsohn Choir of Orchestra London and with the Fagan Singers, a chamber group. Mr. Doncic joined Tsar Lazar as a singer after moving to Pittsburgh in 1992, and 2 years later became the choir's director.

*First Tenor:* Milan Drakulic, John Drzayich, Paul Kochka, George Mistovich, Andy Muha, Michael Oleck, Andrew Talarovich, Miles Vukas **Second Tenor:** Michael M. Hutnik, Dan Jovanovich, Robert Kovacevic, Dennis Lapushanksy, Jim Larkin, Pete Momcilovich, Pero Prpa, Dan Vucelich, Demetrius Yandrich **Baritone:** Nick Jovonovich, Ninko Karas, Paul Karas, Albert Kulics, George Martich, John Martich, Milan Mrkal, Marco Trbovich, Mark Zatezalo, Nick Zatezalo **Bass:** Ted Erdel, Nick Karas, Alex Kavic, Ivan Obrknez, Charles Popovich, David Urban, Gregory Volitich, Chad Wuchenich, John Wuchenich, Mike Wuchenich

Photo courtesy of Tsar Lazar Male Choir.

**A selection of guest vocalists appearing at past SSF Festivals.** This page and opposite page: Top row, left to right: **Vinka Ellesin, Sophia Topalsky, Danitza Ilitsch, Mia Novich,** Middle: **Milan Timotich, Rasha Radenkovich, Uros Seferovich, Militza Kosanchich,** Bottom: **Danica Chirich, Mirko Markovich, Paul Zelich and Milutin Lazich.** Photos courtesy of SSF Archives.

# SERBIAN SINGING FESTIVALS 1936-1999

1936—Akron, Ohio, First Festival
1938—Youngstown, Ohio

1940—Cleveland, Ohio
1948—Pittsburgh, Pennsylvania

1950—Detroit, Michigan
1951—Akron, Ohio
1952—Milwaukee, Wisconsin
1953—Steubenville, Ohio
1954—Gary, Indiana
1955—Cleveland, Ohio
1956—Detroit, Michigan
1957—Steubenville, Ohio
1958—Chicago, Illinois
1959—Johnstown, Pennsylvania

1960—Milwaukee, Wisconsin
1961—Akron, Ohio
1962—Detroit, Michigan
1963—South Chicago
1964—Pittsburgh, Pennsylvania
1965—Milwaukee, Wisconsin
1966—Cleveland, Ohio
1967—Gary, Indiana
1968—Detroit, Michigan
1969—Youngstown, Ohio

1970—Chicago, Illinois
1971—Lackawanna, New York
1972—Gary, Indiana
1973—Cleveland, Ohio
1974—Milwaukee, Wisconsin
1975—Toronto, Ontario, Canada
1976—Akron, Ohio
1977—Detroit, Michigan
1978—Aliquippa, Pennsylvania
1979—Chicago, Illinois

1980—Monroeville, Pennsylvania
1981—Milwaukee, Wisconsin
1982—Chicago, Illinois
1983—Cleveland, Ohio
1984—Joliet, Illinois
1985—Detroit, Michigan
1986—Merrillville, Indiana
1987—Aliquippa, Pennsylvania
1988—Chicago, Illinois
1989—Monroeville, Pennsylvania

1990—South Chicago, Illinois
1991—Windsor, Ontario, Canada
1992—South Bend, Indiana
1993—Pittsburgh, Pennsylvania
1994—Milwaukee, Wisconsin
1995—Chicago, Illinois
1996—Alhambra, California, the First West Coast Festival
1997—Chicago, Illinois
1998—Windsor, Ontario, Canada
1999—Phoenix, Arizona

**SPECIAL FESTIVALS**

1956—The First Canadian Festival, Niagara Falls, Ontario, Canada.
1957—Hamilton, Ontario, Canada.
1958—Windsor, Ontario, Canada.
1967—Special World's Fair Festival, Montreal, Quebec, Canada.

# Serbia: Singing   by Helen Leah Reed, 1916

Serbia, in the hands of a cruel conqueror, stripped of most of her possessions, bereft of happiness, forgotten by her sister nations, had little left but hope. Serbia still cherished a gift inherited from her remote northern ancestors—her gift of song. Her contact with her southern neighbors cheered and strengthened her. She sang and sang, in a minor key, and her mountains reechoed with the deeds of her happier days, with the stories of her heroes, now seeming more splendid because she herself had become so poor and unhappy. For centuries she was like one stunned; she had never been aggressive—now she could not fight against the aggressor who had all the weapons in his own hands.

A younger sister—and poor at that!—a younger sister, who had set out to be perfectly independent—what could she expect? She must work out her own salvation. Besides, she lived so far away from the centers of culture she was almost a barbarian. Yet she was not wholly uncouth. She had been courteous to the Crusaders traversing Europe to crush their common enemy—the Turk; and now the Turk had captured her! Of course it was a pity! It was a busy time in Europe in the 14th and 15th centuries; the nations had enough to do to keep their own houses in order—and when they had leisure they must keep in touch with the new life, with the renaissance of Art and Learning. They were enchanted with the discovery that they were not mere parvenus like distant Serbia, but descendants of that grand old house that had once conquered the world. The beauty of Paganism—ah, that was something worth contemplating! But Serbia—well, the Crusades were over, and the Turk was no longer threatening Western Europe; besides, Serbia had not even belonged to their Church—so what matter if the Turk crushed her? But Serbia was not crushed. Had the nations listened, they could have heard her singing. There was little else she could do, except wait and hope—wait like her Marko for the signal to rise.

Through 5 centuries of subjection to the Turks, the *guslars*, singing the heroic *pesme*, were hardly second in influence to the priests in fortifying the spirits of the suffering Serbs. The intense patriotism of the Serb was kept alive, indeed was often kindled, by the folk songs he had heard even in his cradle. Through all his troubles he has cherished the divine fire of nationality, even as the Vestals conserved the sacred flame.

The Serb, belonging to the most poetical of nations, has the most melodious of all Slav tongues, yet used it as the language of literature a comparatively short time. Even little more than a hundred years ago people were still arguing whether ancient Slavonic or the Serbian vernacular should be the language of literature. But for Dositej Obradovic seen here on the right, this result might have been reached less quickly. He, *"the great sower,"* a notable educator, applied the language of the people to literature, publishing an autobiography, besides poems and treatises, in the common tongue. Before his death in 1811, the *"Write as you speak"* party had won, and literature became the property of the masses. Yet a further improvement in the language was undertaken by Vuk Karadzic, a self-taught cripple, whose grammar, published in 1814, was epochal. He devised the alphabet of 30 letters, each one representing a complete sound, and he published a dictionary and a collection of the *pesme* which he took down from the mouths of the *guslars* who sang them. European diplomats and travelers generations before had brought back accounts of Serbian poetry heard almost as often in those days in foreign countries as in Serbia itself.

Goethe was one of the first to translate them and call attention to those *pesme*. He praised their humor and philosophy, their high heroism mingled with certain spiritual qualities. Soon Sir John Bowring, a skilled linguist, made a translation into English verse which is nearer the original spirit and letter than any that has been made since.

There have also been many fine prose translations of the Kosovo cycle and the other *pesme*, and all readers agree that in them is, as one critic says, *"a clear and inborn poetry, such as can scarcely be found in any other modern people."*

*"Serbian song,"* wrote Schafferik, *"resembles the tone of the violin; old Slavonian, that of the organ; Polish, that of the guitar. The old Slavonian in the Psalms sounds like the loud rush of the mountain stream; The Polish like the sparkling and bubbling of a fountain; and the Serbian like the quiet murmuring of a streamlet in a valley."*

The Serb loves to sing; every young countryman carries his *gusle*, and is ready to use it—a one-stringed violin, shaped something like a mandolin, played on the knee with a bow, like a violoncello. Men and women—peasants and townsmen—all sing. When 2 or more sing together, it is unison and part-singing. The national Serb music is rich in melodies. The traveler today hears the Serb singing a ballad of the days of Tsar Dusan of Kosovo, of the Bulgar War, of Karadjordje (the William Tell of the mountains). The *gusle* wails monotonously, with an occasional trill on one or two minor notes. Some find its music plaintive, others call it tiresome, and travelers as long ago as the beginning of the 18th century have written of seeing numbers of people in a crowd silently weeping as they listened to an old blind man chanting national songs.

There are two great epic cycles—one centering around Tsar Lazar, the other around Marko—and both have to do with the Battle of Kosovo. Fragments of other cycles show that Tsar Dusan, Milos Obilic, and other heroes have been each a chief figure in them. No matter how unlearned, from one point of view, a Serb may be, he can always talk about Stefan Nemanja, or St. Sava, or Marko, and the other great men of his race. Moreover, he is continually creating new songs, new folk lore. In the great mills of this country he lightens his work with his simple melodies. Sometimes the words of his song form a clear narration of the events that brought him to America, even of happenings since his arrival. His own sorrows and his own joys are woven in his epic. After their recent war with Bulgaria, everywhere at village festivals, the Serbs began to sing of their victories—and today they are undoubtedly singing of the sorrows of the past two years.

Mr. Miatovic says that when as cabinet minister he had been defeated, 40 years ago, the next day he heard the people singing this event in the streets. Whatever the subject—whether it deals with ancient times or with the present, whether it is an epic or one of the so-called women's songs—the Serbian *pesma* is anonymous. No single writer or composer claims it. It is the work of the people, all of whom have had a chance to modify it as it has passed through the ages.

*Top, opposite page:* Book jacket of *Serbia, A Sketch* by Helen Leah Reed, 1916—written and published for the benefit of the Serbian Distress Fund, Boston. Courtesy of Archimandrite Dositei Obradovich. *Left, opposite page:* Dositej Obradovic (18th century educator). Illustration by Milan Kecman. *Top:* Filip Vishnic, a guslar who refused to sing songs of praise about the pasha who then blinded him as punishment. Courtesy of Archimandrite Dositei Obradovich. *Above left:* Tsar Lazar. *Right:* Milos Obilic. Illustrations by Milan Kecman.

Among all the heros of the *guslars* the favorite has always been Prince Marko. Although much of the career of Marko in the *pesme* was fabulous, this prince had a real existence in the latter part of the 14th century—the son of Vukasin, who tried to usurp the throne of young Uros after the death of Tsar Dusan and Queen Jelena, unless one prefers to account for Marko's glittering qualities by making him the offspring of a dragon and a fairy queen. He ruled a small territory in Macedonia, and Prilep was his capital. He is said to have died fighting for the sultan. This was after Kosovo, when Serbia was sleeping. Yet he must have had qualities that made him rise above this in popular estimation, for his local reputation grew with time and became national. Certainly for 5 centuries he has been a living personality, not only in Serbian but in Croatian, Bulgarian and Romanian tradition.

Serbian peasants and citizens of a country town, 1867. 19th century engraving courtesy of Archimandrite Dositei Obradovich.

It is worth considering—this theory that in Prince Marko the Serbian nation projects itself; that his sufferings and successes are the sufferings and successes of the whole nation; that it beholds its own virtues and weaknesses in his; its own individuality in his popular personality; its own doom in his tragic fate. Athletic, keen-minded, quickly reading the designs of his foes, he, as an individual, was what Serbia would like to have been as a political entity. Even as he triumphed over Magyar, Venetian or Turk, so would the Serb have triumphed. When Serbia was sunk in poverty the *guslar* brought before his listeners visions of splendid things they could never hope to see, but whose beauties satisfied their imagination.

Marko is the knight without fear, without reproach—the lover of justice, the hater of all oppression. He is kind and dutiful, the protector of the poor and abused. His pity extends even to animals, who in turn often helped him. *"He feared no one but God."* Courteous to all women, tender and dutiful to his mother, Marko could be savage and cruel beyond belief toward the Turks. Human weapons never harmed him, and he weilded a war club weighing 100 pounds, composed of 60 pounds of steel, 30 pounds of silver, and 10 pounds of gold. One touch of this mace beheaded a foe, as one stroke of his saber ripped him open.

Marko's horse, Sarac, his constant companion and helper, was the strongest and swiftest horse ever known. He knew just when to kneel down and save his master from the adversary's lance. He knew how to rear and strike the enemy's charger with his forefeet. When roused, he would spring up 3 lance lengths forward. Glittering sparks flashed from beneath his hoofs, blue flames from his nostrils. He had been known to bite off the ears of the enemy's horse; sometimes he trampled Turkish soldiers to death. Marko fed his horse bread and wine from his own plate. Sarac kept guard over Marko while he slept. He always shared the glory of victory. Yet, whether or not Marko personifies Serbia, in the life of Marko, Serbian medieval life is reflected in this story as an image in a mirror.

In those poems Turks are always unreliable and cruel; Venetians are crafty; the faithless wife is usually lured away by a Turk. In one vivid tale, Marko's own bride, as he is taking her home from Bulgaria, is stolen by a doge of Venice, who, with 300 attendants, had been invited by her father to be part of her bridal procession. His designs do not succeed, and when Marko comprehends this treachery he does not hesitate. *"He cleft the doge's head in twain,"* and he struck another traitor with his saber *"so neatly"* that he fell to earth in 2 pieces.

The touch of exaggeration in all the stories is not one merely of incident but of detail—the kind of exaggeration a child loves. For example, when Marko was brought from the cell where the sultan had imprisoned him for 3 years, his nails were so long that he could plow with them. The Serbs of those days, having few splendid things in their own surroundings, loved to endow Marko with grandeur. On his tent, for instance, was fixed a golden apple. *"In the apple are fixed two large diamonds which shed a light so far and wide that the neighboring tents need no candle at night."* In another instance, a magnificent ring is described—*"so richly studded with precious stones that the whole room was lighted up."*

In these *pesme* one has glimpses not only of all the neighbors who warred upon the Serbians, but of Christian malcontents going over to the Church of Rome or sowing dissensions at home. A careful reader can get an almost complete picture of the Serbian life after the Conquest, painted, to be sure, in high colors.

There are in existence about 38 poems and twice as many prose legends detailing the thrilling exploits of Marko. In spite of certain accounts of his death, it is generally thought that he never died, but withdrew to a cave near the castle of Prilip and is still asleep there. At times, he awakes and looks to see if a sword has come out of a rock where he thrust it to the hilt. When it is out of the the rock, he will know that the time has come for him to appear among the Serbians once more to reestablish the Empire destroyed at Kosovo.

Helen Leah Reed was the author of:
*Napoleon's Young Neighbor* and *Miss Theodora*.

*Above:* A tavern in Dubrovnik, circa 1890. 19th century engravings courtesy of Archimandrite Dositei Obradovich.
*Right:* A Serbian border guard, 1867.

# Vinka

## Born To Sing!

By William Dorich

There are not enough adjectives in the dictionary to properly describe this Serbian superstar. Serbdom in America would be difficult to imagine without the "Queen of Sevdah!" Vinka Ellesin not only made an indelible mark on Serbian culture, she made an incredible contribution to the preservation of Serbian music in the 20th century.

Djoka and Sophia Elesin arrived in America in 1906 from Turija, Backa, and were active members of the Serbian Church. Vinka was born in Akron, Ohio, one of 7 children. She showed a keen interest in music at an early age. The first to awaken each morning, she would sneak downstairs in her nightgown—and while her mother made breakfast for the family—Vinka would stand alongside her father and listened Ilija Miskovich play his prima and sing many songs. Vinka would clasp her hands behind her back and dance the kolo.

At the age of 16, Vinka appeared weekly on Akron radio station WADC in a coast-to-coast broadcast as vocalist with the Jorgovan Orchestra, under the direction of John Halick. Halick brought Vinka to the attention of station owner Al Simmons who arranged a scholarship for Vinka to attend the New York School of Music, but, Vinka's father, who was a very good singer in Yugoslavia where he sang on boat rides on the Tisa River, would have no part of this educational opportunity saying that: *"If Vinka goes to New York, she will forget she is an Ellesin."*

Her father was also determined that his children would only speak Serbian in the home. This was of great benefit to Vinka's singing career. Her infallible accent and perfect Serbian diction astounded new emigrants to this country who were amazed to discover that she was born in the United States.

Years later in a Voice of America interview, Vinka was asked what inspired her to take up *'sevdalinka'* singing. She responded that her mentor was Sofka, a famous singer in Yugoslavia who happened to be listening to the broadcast that day. She wrote to Vinka and expressed her gratitude at being the *"American Sofka's"* mentor.

Vladimir (Vlajko) Lugonja, founder of the Serbian Singing Federation, visited Akron as a guest of Arkadija Velemirovic where he met Vinka and heard her sing alongside a Victrola. He immediately detected in her a rare talent. He praised her singing and advised her to continue singing and predicted that one day she would be the leading Serbian singer of *sevdalinkas* in America. At this time Vinka was still in public school.

Years later in 1962, Vladimir Lugonja wrote in Vinka's autograph book: *"To Vinka, the Queen of Sevdalinka! I am proud and happy to have discovered you as a teenager. I'll never forget, nor will I ever regret the day I crowned you 'Queen of Sevdah' in Akron, Ohio. Many years may you reign!"*

One day in Cleveland, a speeding car was stopped by the police. The driver explained that he was in a hurry and that the police should provide him with an escort. After they arrived at the other end of the city, the car came to a stop at 3839 Payne Avenue. The officer got out of his squad car and said: *"Say, buddy, this is the Black Whale."* The driver replied: *"Sure, officer, but haven't you heard? Vinka's back in town!"* Vinka appeared every Friday, Saturday and Sunday, singing the songs from the time of the pashas and Serbian songs which touched the heart. For the Black Whale, Vinka made guest appearances in Detroit, Chicago and throughout the East and Midwest. Vinka's vibrant voice, outstanding on its own, was accompanied by her body language that became her trademark. She invented *"soul food"*— the kind that feeds the spirit.

One evening in 1938, Sammy Kaye, a top band leader in the country, stopped by the Black Whale and was so overwhelmed by Vinka's singing that he wanted her to replace his vocalist who was leaving his orchestra.

The next day, Professor Charles De Herrick, without telling Vinka, took her to radio station WTAM where she was introduced to

At the Blue Danube in Detroit, second from right, Dave Zupkovich. Photo courtesy of Ann Pollock.

Sammy Kaye. He wanted Vinka to audition for him. When he asked her if she could sing any popular American songs, Vinka replied, *"Yes!, I can sing the Star Spangled Banner,"* That was not quite what Sammy Kaye had in mind. He provided her with musical arrangements and set up a recording session for the following week. Vinka decided not to show up for that session, sensing that her mission in life was to promote Serbian songs and to entertain Serbian audiences. How blessed we are that she had such intuition.

The name Vinka became a household word. She was booked every week for more than 35 years and she made 36 records. Her singing ability came naturally to her and she never let her audience down.

In 1947 on her own Sevdalinka Record label, Vinka recorded 2 albums with Steve Pavlekovich and his orchestra. In the late 1950s, Vinka recorded with Marty Kapugi and his orchestra featuring Mel Dokich on the violin. Vinka spent the war years in Detroit, where she sang at the Blue Danube, the Russian Samovar and Jim's Cabaret. She sang at countless Serbian picnics and concerts throughout the United States, at fund raising functions whose proceeds went for the purchase of Victory Bonds, for the aid of General Draza Mihailovich and his Chetnik forces and for the American Red Cross relief work in Yugoslavia.

Many Serbian mothers brought their sons to Vinka's concerts and night club appearances, where she would dedicate *Moj Milane kad u vojsku podjes* (My Milan, When You Go Into The Army) to these young men headed off to defend democracy.

Vinka moved to California in 1959, where she first entered the travel business in Santa Barbara. By 1966 she owned her own successful travel service in Ventura, California.

Vinka appeared at countless Church, SNF, KSS, SSF and other charitable functions. A priest was once overheard saying, *"Vinka provided many churches and halls with the bricks when the going was tough."* Once in Gary, Indiana, at Sarajevsko Vece, she was such a hit that requests poured in from 8 p.m. to 2 a.m. The Popovich Brothers were kept frantically busy playing every request. The audience just would not let her stop. In 1947 at the SSF Victory Festival held at the Monastery grounds in Libertyville, Illinois, over 7,000 people came to hear the Serbian choirs of America sing praises to the glory of God and to pay homage to their Serbian heritage. In 1974, Vinka was crowned *"Queen of Sevdalinka"* by the Tamburitza Extravaganza Association of America and was inducted into the Tamburitza Association's Hall of Fame in 1976.

The famous Sophie Tucker, remembered for her rendition of *One of These Days,* was popular at the Florentine Gardens in Los Angeles in 1947, a night club as popular at the Coconut Grove, boasted before her retirement that she was singing to her third generation. Vinka sang to her fourth generation and will be an inspiration to future Serbian generations. But none of this remarkable story should come as a surprise, as Vinka was born to sing!

*Right:*
Formal portrait, photo courtesy of *The American Srbobran.*
*Below:*
Vinka singing with the Popovich Brothers at a picnic. Photo courtesy of Adam Popovich.

*Orchestras in which Vinka sang:*

The Isidor Bajich Orchestra • Banat • Beograd • Biser • Dragic Blagojevich • Djura Bogicevich • Blue Danube • Crlenica Brothers • Djoka Dokich • Mel Dokich • Lex Ellesin • Emil Grecni • Mel Evanovich and his Balkan Serenaders • John Halick • Raja Jankovich • The Jorgovan Orchestra • Javor • Marty Kapugi and the Sar Planina • Vojkan Kalenich • Baca Kiurski and the Drina Orchestra • Tilly Klaich and the Balkan Serenaders • Danny Kukich • Teddy Kukich • Danilo Kozarski • The Lira Orchestra •Mirko Markovich • Plavi Mesec • Ilija Miskovich • Stasa Milanovich • Emil Monroe • Neven • The Panayatovich Brothers • Steve Pavlekovich • Deda Petrovich • Mica Petrovich • The Popovich Brothers • Djoka Pribich • Ceda Radovanovich • The Serbian Radio Orchestra • Srpski Seljaci • George Skrbina • The Zora Orchestra • Zora • Dave Zupkovich

**Highlights of Vinka's Life**

**October 17, 1935**
American Srbobran reports another Serbian radio program on WJAY in Akron, Ohio featuring Miss Vinka and the Tamburitza Drustvo "Yorgovan."

**December 3, 1939**
The Njegosh Choir of Cleveland celebrates its 10th Anniversary. Constantine Fotich, Royal Yugoslav Minister to the U.S.A., was guest of honor.

**December 7, 1941**
The Odbor Srpskih Drustava of Detroit holds a concert. On the program are Vinka Ellesin, Uros Seferovich and Edo Lubich. During the concert a bulletin is received that the Japanese have attacked Pearl Harbor.

**July 20, 1942**
Over $5,000 is donated at Draza Mihailovich Day in Detroit, which featured the Ravanica Choir, Vinka Ellesin, Stanko Plavsich and Ljubica Grkovich.

**May 9, 1943**
Vinka sings in South Chicago at the 450th Anniversary of the establishment of the printing press at Obod, sponsored by the Crnogorski Prosvetni Klub.

**November 28, 1943**
Vinka makes her first West Coast appearance at the Los Angeles Breakfast Club. Other appearances follow in San Pedro and other Pacific communities.

**September 22, 1946**
The Jedinstvo Club of Weirton, West Virginia presents Vinka in concert. Also on the program, Capt. Nick Lalich with his war slides of General Mihailovich and his Chetnik forces.

**October 2, 1949**
Bishop Nikolai Velimirovich lays the cornerstone of the Indiana Harbor Memorial Hall dedicated to the veterans of World War II. Vinka and the *Sar Planina* orchestra headline the program.

**October 21, 1956**
The first Canadian SSF Festival is held in Niagara Falls, Ontario, Canada. Vinka appears as guest after returning from European tour.

# A Living Legend – The Popovich Brothers

by Manuel Trbovich and Ed Levine - 1975

**1901** A Serbian peasant widow in a small village in Lika bid farewell to her teen-aged son whom she would never see again. Life in the village had been cruelly austere, and the future held nothing better in sight. She felt she must urge her son to go out into the world in search of a better life. With no industrial skill or experience, young Nikola Popovich went to Germany in search of employment. The fact that he had not learned to read or write did not discourage him in the least and he soon found employment on the German railroads.

**1902** After working for a year, Nikola journeyed to the United States. With other immigrants he was herded into a box car and shipped to the Midwest—working for a short while on the railroads in Michigan, earning his way through Missouri and westward into Colorado. There he began work as a silver miner. To the scattered Serb immigrants of Colorado, Denver was like a friendly oasis. Here old friends would gather to exchange greetings and visit—and it was here that Nikola met Ljubica, who was to remain at his side for the rest of her life. Together they suffered many hardships, but their relationship was blessed by many children and that is what this story is all about.

**1908** The young couple made Denver their home. Nikola worked on the railroads and in the coal and silver mines, while Ljubica kept house and took care of the oldest daughter, Vietta. The little family was struck by tragedy in 1907, when the first son died in early infancy. In 1908 Eli was born, followed by Adam in 1909.

**1911** By the time Ted was born in 1911, the family had moved to Globeville, Colorado, and shortly thereafter they moved to the copper flats of Nevada—where Nikola went to work in the copper mines. It was in the little mining town of Veteran, Nevada that daughter Eva was born in 1913.

The State Miner's Literacy Law forced the family to leave Nevada and move to the Utah mining camps, and it was during this period that son Marko was born in 1915. Subsequently, this anti-immigrant law was repealed and the family returned to Ruth, Nevada, where, in 1917, another

**1917** son was born but died before reaching his first birthday.

Ljubica and Nikola Popovich, the parents.

Photos courtesy of Adam Popovich.

The little Nevada community had no Serbian, Greek or Russian Orthodox churches, and the task of making the children aware of their religious heritage fell to Ljubica. She knew all the Serbian holidays and saw to it that Easter, Christmas and Krsna Slava were days of joy and celebration. Savin Dan was a very special observance, and all the Serbian children of the neighborhood were taught recitations. The only instrumental music available then was provided by the traditional gusle. To fill the musical gap, all the children were taught to sing.

From their mother, the boys learned to read and write in the Cyrillic alphabet before they reached grammar school age. Nikola, their father, being unable to read or write, relied heavily on his virtually faultless memory to teach his children the beautiful music he had learned as a boy. During the fall and winter evenings, and after a hard day's work at the mines, Nikola would gather his children by the light of a coal oil lamp and sing epic poems to them. From memory, he sang line after line and verse after endless verse of the heroic deeds of the old Serb heroes. This is how his boys learned of Kraljevic Marko, Milos Obilic, Toplica Milan, and the "Devet Jugovicha."

"Tiha Noci" was the first song they learned from their father. During play time hours, while other boys in the community imagined themselves to be cowboys, the Popovich sons took on the roles of Kraljevic Marko, Milos Obilic, and Tzar Lazar. Although Nikola was not musically inclined, he did play a samica or danguba, an instrument with all strings tuned alike. There was a primitive beauty to the sound of this instrument accompanying the moving old melodies he sang.

For the Christmas holidays the children of the neighborhood would go carolling. There were the Kalajdjia boys, their first cousins, the Grubich boys, and Mele Delich, sister of Helen Delich Bentley, former congresswoman. During this holiday season, the Popovich household resounded with happy singing voices of men, women and children.

These were war years, however, and even the isolated little mining town of Ruth, Nevada, did not escape untouched by the conflict. Serbia was under attack by the mighty armies of the Austro-Hungarian Empire, and young immigrant Serbs responded to a call for help by offering themselves as volunteers. When they left to fight for Serbian freedom, friends and relatives gathered to give these brave men a ceremonial send-off. It was in the closing months of the war that the youngest brother, Pete, was born. He was followed by sister Mila, born in 1920.

The spring of 1924 found the struggling Popovich family living in the little coal mining camp of Pictou, Colorado. Word was that 5 miles away over a rugged hill, appropriately called "Hogback," there was a man teaching youngsters to play tambura. Eli and Ted hiked across the hill to join up. Adam followed a short while later, but Marko, affectionately known as "Mikie," was kept at home, being considered too young for this adventure. The 3 older boys hiked back and forth across old "Hogback" 3 and 4 times a week to receive their lessons from the late George Kachar, a fine man of great patience, especially with youngsters.

However, young "Mikie" was not to be denied— and, when his older brothers practiced at home, he played along with them and in a very short time he surpassed the 10 charter members of the tambura class.

Ljubica had great faith in the musical talents of her children. On one occasion she borrowed 15 dollars to purchase a violin from a Yugoslav orchestra leader. Why a violin? No one in her household played one or expressed any interest in one, but in her ever active imagination she surmised that as

Photo courtesy of Helen Popovich.

The charter members of the tambura class of George Kachar in Walsenburg, Colorado, 1921. Photo courtesy of Del Casher.

long as the violin was around, sooner or later, someone would become interested in it—and indeed, it came to pass that Adam developed an interest and, for a while, took violin lessons. For some time afterward he actually played the lead music for the group on his violin.

For many years, Ljubica kept pointing out to her hard working husband that it was futile to remain in the coal fields. In her view, the mines held no future for any member of the family. Nikola finally agreed, and in 1927 moved his family to Pueblo, Colorado. This was a long economic step forward for the family, for here in Pueblo stood the imposing smoke stacks of the Colorado Fuel and Iron Company—the only complete steel mill west of the Mississippi. Nikola went to work there immediately and was followed by Eli and Adam.

It was while the family lived in Pueblo that sister Eva with her fine, full soprano voice won a state music school contest. After some tutoring by her brothers, she learned to play the kontrashica and joined the group along with a fifth brother, Pete, who was coached on the bugarija. The family musical group boasted 6 members now, and they appeared for 3 nights at Maccabee's Fete, complete with display photos. Regrettably, none of the photos was preserved.

Their repertoire included Serbian music, marches, overtures, and popular songs. Their remarkable talents won them inspiring recognition when they were awarded a five-night stand at the Rialto Theatre in Pueblo. However, they now had a far more ambitious venture in mind—a tour of the Western states!

The idea of such a trip was advanced by a veteran tamburash, Milan Vurdelja. Vurdelja had come from Gary, Indiana—where he played with Jovo Crljenica and his sons, George and Vaso. The Crljenicas were held in high esteem among the lovers of tambura music. Being a man of some skill with hammer and saw, Vurdelja built a special trailer which would transport the group's clothes and equipment—which now included new riding boots in place of the white stockings. In the center of the trailer he built an ingenious slide compartment to house the berda (bass) in such a way that it could be strapped down to prevent it from bouncing around.

## THE FIRST TOUR—1928

The group bought a sophisticated, secondhand 1924 Ford sedan with a "Ruxle Axle," which was an added power drive with a stick shift. The "Tin Lizzie," as the Fords were called in those days, drew the ambitious assignment of pulling the loaded trailer, the 4 Popovich brothers, and Vurdelja, a stocky man of 230 pounds. And this was to be done over highways which for many miles consisted of unpaved roads graded with crushed stone.

Armed with only 100 dollars in cash and a million dollars of enthusiasm, the touring tamburashi took off in May of 1928, heading for Denver and Northern Colorado. There was no advance man for this tour—in fact, there was no advance notice of any kind. It was only upon arrival that the promotion began.

All went well throughout Northern Colorado—but as the troupe moved toward Wyoming, a speeding car came smashing into the "Tin Lizzie," interrupting the tour. Needless to say, the group's treasury was seriously depleted by the time the necessary repairs were made. By the time they reached Rock Springs, Wyoming, the 5 weary musicians had 2 dollars among them. Things could not have looked worse.

From Nevada, the touring Ford bumped along into California, making stops in San Pedro, Los Angeles and Sacramento. In Los Angeles, the musicians visited the Crljenica family, those tambura pioneers who had given them their childhood inspiration during a stopover in Nevada in 1917.

In Sacramento they stayed with their cousins, the Kalajdjia family—Mrs. Kalajdjia was their tetka, their mother's sister. From California they went to Portland, Seattle, Spokane, Aberdeen, and Vancouver. In Seattle, they were guests of the U. S. Navy on two occasions. In the first instance, they were taken aboard the U. S. battleship "Colorado," no small treat for young men from the coal fields. The tour moved eastward through Kellog, Idaho, and into Butte, Montana, home of the world's deepest copper mine and many Serb miners. After a pause in Yellowstone National Park, a second visit was made in Rock Springs, Wyoming before going to Nebraska, Kansas, Missouri, Iowa, Peoria, Gary and Indiana Harbour. Although it was not planned, the tour ended in South Chicago. Serbian songs and dances had been brought to many isolated communities, many of which had never heard a tambura group. It is interesting to note that in some of the communities along the tour the concerts were sponsored by Croatian clubs and organizations. Everywhere, the response was warm and overwhelming from everyone.

The tour reached South Chicago in October, 1928, which was intended to be a stop like all the others. The *"Boys"* rented an apartment which was furnished only with beds, a kitchen table, and some chairs. This was to be the headquarters from which they would go to the playing jobs in the surrounding communities. Unlike the Western communities, the Serb colonies in the Midwest were, by contrast, heavily populated and before long the *"Boys"* were being booked for various affairs. One of the memorable jobs was playing for the celebration of the consecration of the Joliet church in November, 1928.

In December of that year the Serbian Singing Society, Sloboda, held its annual concert and dance. *"Bach"* Rotkovich, who, with his father and his brother, was engaged to play for this occasion, was unable to play his *brach* because he had broken his hand playing football. The desperate musicians prevailed upon Adam to help them. Adam responded by substituting on the *brach* for Bach, beginning a relationship with the Sloboda Choir that has lasted to this day. Adam joined the choir that evening, and the following Friday he brought Eli and Ted along to the rehearsal. Adam and Ted have been members ever since.

In January of 1929, the rest of the Popovich family joined the boys in Chicago—bringing with them their newest infant daughter, Mary. That year came the Crash of 1929 with the accompanying economic disaster. Adam and Eli, who had been working in the steel mills, were laid off along with thousands of others. Playing jobs, now desperately needed, trickled in. However, the pay was a mere pittance, sometimes as little as 10 or 15 dollars, and many times the *"pay"* was only a promise to pay. Many jobs of playing for the Church and various organizations were done free of charge. For the Popovich family times were doubly difficult because there were so many of them—nevertheless, they pulled through those difficult years thanks to the efforts of some very good people in the Serbian community. Among happier events of the time were the 4th of July and Labor Day picnics in Libertyville. Playing there was unique, since no one group held center stage. Instead, a different musical group played under every big tree. This was most exciting for the Popovich brothers, for it afforded them the chance to see and hear the popular tambura *"greats"* of that period. Among them were lliya Miskovich, Vlade Marianovich, Djoko Dokich, as well as accordionist Milan Panchevac. While the Boys were inspired by the singing and playing of the *"greats,"* those old-timers in turn were fascinated by the authenticity and quality of the Popovich brothers' singing and playing, particularly the prima playing of brother Marko.

Barn Dance Photo courtesy of Mitzi Alexich.

> *"It took a World War to break up the Popovich Brothers."*

In that same year Sloboda held its first *"Barn Dance."* This spectacular event was made possible mainly because of the participation of the Popovich Brothers, who provided the necessary accompaniment for the performers. The only lead instrument then available was Marko's prima, and it was Marko's incredible knack for accompaniment which paved the way for all the successful *"Barn Dances"* in the ensuing years.

The year 1933 marked Chicago's observance of *"A Century of Progress,"* during which time the Popovich Brothers performed in many different parts of the World's Fair. The climax came in July when a huge *"Yugoslav Day"* celebration was organized at Soldier's Field. Ten thousand spectators turned out and sat through a drizzling rain to see and hear Serbian, Croatian, and Slovenian tambura groups, choirs, and kolo groups. The highlight was a massive tambura group with representation from all parts of the country. It was Adam Popovich who drew the honor of directing this inspiring performance.

Adam's musical interest grew immensely during this period, having received much of his broader training from Sloboda's choirmaster, Joseph Kind, who was a well-schooled musician in every respect. From him, Adam learned piano, harmony, and composition. In 1936 Mr. Kind expressed a desire to retire, and George Lalich, Sloboda's founding president, had stepped down, so the choir was now left without a director and a president. No one was eager to accept the presidency, but when the nomination turned to Eli, he agreed to accept, only if Adam would become the director. Adam agreed, and—with the exception of 2 relatively short interruptions—he was Sloboda's director until he retired in 1997. Throughout the years of 1936 to 1940, the Popovich Brothers made many trips to various cities and states. All of this, of course, was done over week-ends, for all of the Boys earned their livelihoods at other jobs. Eli, Marko and Pete were ironworkers, while Adam and Ted worked in the steel mills.

## THE SECOND TOUR—1940

A 6 month tour of the Western states was launched. This time the tour, which included brother Pete, was in sharp contrast to the 1928 venture. There were new costumes, new programs, a custom-made trailer, and, above all, a 1939 Buick. Following almost the same path as the 1928 tour, they stopped twice in memorable Rock Springs, Wyoming—as they had done in 1928. As before, the receptions were warm and enthusiastic—and Milwaukee was the last scheduled concert before the *"homecoming."* During the stay there, they registered for the draft, without giving a thought to what was to follow this step.

The group returned to South Chicago in the Fall of 1940 for a triumphal homecoming reception, and in time to play for sister Mila's wedding. The tour then moved through Indiana, Ohio, Pennsylvania and West Virginia, regaling all who heard them with moving tamburitza melodies.

With the successful tour behind them, the *"Boys"* returned to South Chicago, their mood now one of returning to *"normalcy"* for a while before contemplating the next move. The next move, however, was made for them when the United States entered World War II. Brother Pete was swept into the Army and within a month was shipped to the South Pacific without even the customary 10 days leave. Eli entered the Army Corps of Engineers. These were sad days for the family, but they were encouraged by the parting words of

The "Boys." Seated is Pete Mistovich.
Photos courtesy of Adam Popovich.

brother Eli who reminded them that *"it took a World War to break up the Popovich Brothers."*

The turn of events was a cruel blow to their mother, whose health was failing rapidly. She died in 1943, leaving them with her precious legacy. She taught them by her own example that no matter how difficult and trying the times may be one can always find the means to welcome guests, assist friends and relatives —and above all, preserve the Serbian cultural heritage. Eventually, brother Marko entered the Navy, and he, too, was sent to the South Pacific, while brother Eli, now an OSS officer, was sent to Europe. Of the original 5 brothers, only Adam and Ted were left at home—and they now had to find a way to keep the music going. Thanks to camaraderie among the Chicago tamburashi, they found willing support, and substitutes were enlisted for the absent brothers; the music went on throughout the war years.

**THE POST WAR YEARS**
The end of World War II was great news to the Popovich family, for it was triply great because word came that the 3 absent brothers were alive and well and would soon return. In due time, Eli, Marko, and Pete came home to the welcoming embrace of the family. Not long afterward, Pete, the youngest brother, moved on to Pennsylvania—where he lived for many years.

The 4 older brothers decided to go into business on the southeast side of Chicago and opened a tavern/ nightclub called *"Club Selo."* As the name implied, this was no ordinary nightclub. Its motif was Eastern European. The cuisine featured *"sarma"* (stuffed cabbage) and other Serbian specialities; while the entertainment, of course, was provided by the Popovich Brothers, although, on occasion, other groups were featured. Among those were Marty Kapugi's *"Sar Planina"* and Dave Zupkovich with his Balkan Orchestra.

The atmosphere at Club Selo was friendly and jovial. Serbs, Croatians and people of various European backgrounds flocked to hear the Popovich Brothers play— and Club Selo was great fun for the patrons. It is now a pleasant memory to the many people who met there regularly and who still talk about those unforgettable evenings.

Brother Eli now returned to government service; this time on a permanent basis. This left Adam, Ted and Marko with the problem of finding a full-time replacement—and they turned to one of the *"pinch hitters,"* Pete Mistovich, who measured up to the challenge beyond expectations.

For the next period, the orchestra's pace was deliberately held down and only occasional long trips were made. It was time now to do something about the long overdue task of setting the music to records. Through the late 60s and early 70s, 5 albums and 5 stereo tapes were produced.

Special recognition came in July of 1973 when the Smithsonian Institute invited the Popovich Brothers Tamburitza Orchestra to participate in the *Festival of American Folk-life.* The group was flown to Washington to perform for 2 days on the mall between the Washington and Lincoln Memorials. While performing there, they had the opportunity to meet and visit with the finest tamburashi (including Janika Balaz and the Radio Novi Sad Tamburitza Orchestra) of Yugoslavia who also participated in the festival. Also performing from New York was Tillie Klaich and his Balkan Serenaders and Joe Grcevich and his talented group from Pennsylvania. After performing at the prestigious affair, the Popovich Brothers were officially inducted into the *Tamburitza Hall of Fame.*

**A FAMILY AFFAIR**
To be able to play continuously for 70 years calls for enthusiasm, stamina and courage on the part of the musicians. Yet, there was another vital element, the support from family members not directly involved in the music. The wives and sisters of the Popovich Brothers played a crucial role in holding together and encouraging the musical group. What is not generally known is the fact that there were as many Popovich daughters as there were sons.

The oldest sister, Vietta Knez, resided with her husband, Dmitar, in Tucson, Arizona before both passed away. Their sons, Bob, Nick and Fred lived nearby before they died. The youngest son, Jimmy lives outside Springfield Missouri.

Photo courtesy of Adam Popovich.

Another sister, Mila Trbovich, and husband, Mane, resided in Hammond, Indiana—until Mila passed away in 1981. Mane died in California in 1991, where he had moved after remarrying. Their son Marco lives in Pittsburgh and their daughter Yovonne (Mrs. Sam) Orlich, live in Mariville, Indiana. A third sister, Sophie Ostoich, still lives in South in Pittsburgh and their daughter Yvonne (Mrs. Sam) Orlich, live in Merrillville, Indiana. A third sister, Sophie Ostoich, still lives in South Chicago, with her son Ted. Her husband Milan died in 1997. Their daughter, Ljubica Hayden lives with her husband John and their 4 sons in nearby Lansing. Daughter Martha, son-in-law Butch Tesich and their son Nikolas live in surburan Detroit. The baby sister, Mary Stampr, lives in Lockport, Illinois not far from her daughters Diane Huber, Joan Lasky, and Christine Book. Mary's husband George passed away this year. Popovich daughter, Eva Cummings, seen below, was the mother of major baseball player, Eli Grba. She was killed in the 1972 Chicago commuter train crash that took 45 lives.

Sisters Mary, Sophie, Eva, Mila, Vietta and father Nikola, 1960s.

In 1969 Sophie Popovich, wife of Adam, passed away after a long illness. She was the first to take leave of the adult family circle. Nikola Popovich died in the fall of 1976, not long after his son Marko's passing. He was 95 years old. Marko was the group's perfectionist and its severest critic, and he constantly drove the group toward improvement until his untimely passing in 1976. His wife, Helen, lives in Chicago near her youngest daughter Diane Zec, her husband Dan and their 3 children. Their other daughter Vietta (Mrs. Bob Fuller) live in San Leandro, California as do their children.

Serbian immigrants in North America, like their ancestors, were rugged people accustomed to adversity. Their folk songs, consequently, were songs of eagles and falcons, of majestic mountains and awesome forests, of strong horses and brave warriors and of healthy sons and sturdy fathers. Songs such as these had to be sung by singers whose voices projected strength and virility. Nowhere was there a singer who could fulfill such demanding requirements better than Ted Popovich. Year after year this profoundly masculine voice rocked the Serbian halls around the country. For many of those years he sang with no help from microphones and amplifiers. A man of incredible stamina, he endures gruelling demands upon the vocal chords. Ted had many great moments in his singing career, but perhaps his greatest came when Adam and the Sloboda Choir recorded *"Orao klikce."* It was in this performance that Ted brought forth *"Niko nema sto Srbin imade."* It was the first serious recording of that number and it swept the country like a brush fire. With this song, as with so many others he sang over the years, Ted inspired more young people to sing than has any other Serbian singer. Ted and his wife, Mildred, live in Chicago. Their daughter Natalie (Mrs. Milan) Peinovich lives in Hickory Hills, Illinois. One of their daughters, Danella (Mrs. Bob) Winovich, resides in Pittsburgh. Their daughter Dorine, a beautiful soprano in her own right, died in 1995—she was only 58.

Serbian music cannot be judged by contemporary popular standards, for it has a quality that transcends both lyrics and melody. There is a common thread that runs through all the songs, be they songs of life or death; war or peace; fields and mountains, or of love. All transmit a spirit that is quickly sensed by anyone of Serbian background. They tell him who he is and from where he came, they give him that exhilarating feeling of having an unmistakable identity in a world where many are so rapidly losing theirs.

The Popovich Brothers and their music carried this spirit to many corners of this continent. Generations of Serbs will cherish the invaluable contribution which this remarkable group of men have made to preserving their cultural values and traditions. Enthusiasm for music of the Popovich Brothers is as widespread today as it has been at any time. People still flock to hear them in person, ready to crowd around the tambura the moment Ted opens up with the familiar Ej from Niko nema. Whenever there is an announcement of a forthcoming affair, there is always a pleasant anticipation when the bottom line reads:

"Music by the Popovich Brothers."

# Tamburitza ...
## Serbian Music in 20th Century America

by William Dorich

Serbs and their Orthodox Church are synonymous. So, too, are Serbs and tamburitza music. The first Serbian Orthodox church built on this continent was established in Jackson, California, in 1894. Those original Serbian settlers brought with them the customs of the Serbian culture. For more than a century, the sons and daughters of those early pioneers preserved Serbian music in the United States—their legacy binds previous generations to the present. Their incredible gift was the wisdom to preserve their music for the future.

Ethnic cultures are identified more readily by the instruments they play than the music that emanates from them. Mention the *balalaika* and immediately people know you are talking about Russian folk music—or the *bouzouki*, which quickly identifies that of the Greeks.

The Belgrade Choral Society, which began in 1853, had only 88 years to perfect Serbian music before the Second World War. The phenomenon that surrounded tamburitza music peaked in the Balkans prior to that war and included years of tambura music on Belgrade radio under the direction of Alexander Aranicki (shown on p. 81). The popularity of Serbian music plummeted under Tito's Communist system that tried to destroy ethnic individuality by a forced harmony called *"Yugoslavism."* Broz Tito, a Croat, also tried to homogenize the people of the Balkans, only to discover that, like oil and water, when the shaking stopped, the separation was immediate.

The Serbs in America, arriving before the turn of the century, and those who continued to flee oppression at the end of two World Wars, had managed to preserve their tamburitza experience. The revival of tamburitza music today in Serbia can be directly attributed to the popularity of the music among the Serbs in the diaspora, particularly in the United States.

Author's Note:

In the book, *A History of the Tambura—Vol. II, The Tambura In America* by Walter Kolar, published in 1975 by Duquesne University's Folk Arts Department in Pittsburgh, Pennsylvania Mr. Kolar writes:

***"Very little concrete evidence has been found to give vent to the idea that the tambura was being played in America at any time prior to the year 1900."***

Music scholars are surely mused at such an irresponsible comment considering that Serb immigrant musicians arriving on this continent as early as 1879 in the Gold Country of Jackson, California, and brought with them their Tambura instruments and where Serbian Christians established the St. Sava Church organization in Amador County in 1886 and built their first Serbian Orthodox church on this continent in 1894. Advertisements in newspapers printed in 1895 offered ***"Tambura instruments for sale manufactured by the Dobranic and Vardian Co. of Cleveland, Ohio."*** Mr. Kolar's remark implies that Serbian craftsmen were in the United States making tambura instruments for 5 years prior to 1900, but no one was buying or playing them—leading this writer to wonder how Dobranic and Vardian Co. managed to remain in business for so many years? A recently discovered 1895 catalogue from Dobranic and Vardian Co. claims that the company had received letters from *"2,000 grateful customers who appreciated their fine craftsmanship."*

Dozens of highly respected Serbian orchestras through 1975 were omitted from *A History of the Tambura*? Kolar's remark appears self-serving as he goes on to cite *"The first Croatian orchestra, Hrvatska Banda Ban Jelacic of Duquense in 1910"* (shown here). However, this image clearly shows a brass band of the old German style and not tamburitza. History and scholarship are ill served when 97% of the Serbian tamburitza orchestras of this century were omitted from Walter Kolar's book and equally insensitive that Serbian musicians were ignored by Duquesne University's ethnomusicology department in a city with a rather large and active Serbian population?

Only three Serbian orchestras were included in the book, *"Tambura in America"* they were the Popovich Brothers, Crljenica Brothers and Srpski Oro ... and for obvious reasons. The Popovich Brothers were inducted into the Tamburitza Hall of Fame in 1973, two years before Mr. Kolar wrote his book and difficult to ignore a Serbian orchestra of such national prominence. Also difficult to omit was the Crljenica Brothers who played in such Academy Award-winning motion pictures as Lawrence of Arabia and Dr. Zhivago. And finally, hard to ignore was the orchestra Srpski Oro in 1909, a name that means "Serbian Eagle," founded a year before Mr. Kolar's reference to the "first" Croatian orchestra of 1910.

At the height of Serbian immigration to the United States in the late 1870s was at a time of composers like Josif Marinkovic and Stevan Mokranjac when tamburitza music was being played in Serbia. The likelihood that "no tamburitza music was being played before 1910" by Serbian immigrants for nearly 20 years is a question of historical accuracy. At the dedication of the St. Sava Church in Jackson in 1894, records reveal that ***"tamburitza music was played."***

This section of the book is devoted to remembering those Serbian musicians whose contributions to tamburitza music in America have very deep roots. Worth mentioning is the fact that a number of the Serbian orchestras, detailed in the following pages, had Croatian, Hungarian, Russian and Slovenian members—revealing the multi-ethnic diversity within the Serbian communities in the United States. In this limited space I am attempting to present an overview of Serbian Tamburitza in the past century. My omissions have been based on the space allotted. I apologize if the history of your favorite orchestra or individual performer has not been recounted.

Hrvatska Banda 'Ban Jelacic,' Duquesne, Pennsylvania, 1910. Ban, the word meaning (Governor) Jelacic was head of Banovina Hrvatska, the Croatian municipality under Austro-Hungarian rule in the 19th century—he was known as a Serbophobe. The main square in Zagreb, Croatia is named *Trg Bana Jelacica* in honor of this man.

*Below:* Belgrade Radio Tambura.
Director Alexander Aranicki
(1940). Photo courtesy
Mokranjac School of Music, Belgrade.
*Middle*: George Skrbina, 1966.
*Top Right:* Tony Markulin, Rudy Skrbina,
Lou Markulin, Steve Markulin and
George Skrbina, 1945.
Photos courtesy of Ann Prementine.
Bottom Far Right: Nicholas Vasich, 1923.
Photo courtesy of Mila Miller.

It is difficult to ignore such turn of the century craftsmen as Nicholas Vasich (shown above), a Serb, born in Zvornik, Bosnia, who came to the United States and was building the highest quality violins in the early 1920s for such superstars as Rubinoff, Kreisler, Elman and Spalding. A child of poverty, Nicholas Vasich became a ward of "Privrednik," an old Serbian institution for indigent children in Bosnia. He was given commercial training and placed in an apprenticeship. Vasich studied under the tutelage of such masters as Jan Dvorak of Bohemia. He also studied and worked with the leading violin makers of Russia and Germany prior to coming to the United States.

George Skrbina was born in Pulpelsa, Yugoslavia in 1906. He left his mark on tamburitza music in America. If you believe his story you no doubt believe that he bought his first instrument by selling eggs. He is best known for putting Youngstown, Ohio on the map as a key locale for tamburitza music and passing on his knowledge to generations of young people. His business acumen went far beyond selling eggs, and George Skrbina became a contractor in addition to operating a hotel and a well-known cocktail lounge called the Jolly Bar. One of his young students, Libby Fill, got an early start on the woman's liberation movement by forming her own all-female Serbian orchestra. Over the years, George Skrbina maintained his friendship with fellow musicians from his orchestra—Paul Adamovich, Steve Bellish, Mel Evanovich, John Kracanic, Joe Marmilich, Matt Nenkovich, Roy Rasheta, and Pete Vladkovich. George died in 1967 and at his funeral, a combined group of musicians played at the gravesite—the most profound honor musicians can bestow on each other.

Libby's Girls, however, could be considered late bloomers when it comes to the women's lib in America —if you consider the 1898 photograph of Theresa Hegyi shown with her brothers before the turn of the century. In 1909 Theresa Hegyi was featured on prima in The Balkan Orchestra. Her scrollhead was fitted with friction violin pegs for tuners—a common practice at the time. Women's tamburitza groups are fondly remembered in California, particularly the Vaso Crljenica Orchestra during WWII—which included 19 women. The history of tamburitza music in America includes such gifted women as Alexandra Djeorgevich, Vinka Ellesin, Olga Kolman, Martha Kukich, Bernadette Luketich, Mia Novich, Violet Panajatovich, Gorica Popovich, Dawn Radicevich, Evica Rapaich, Seka Senich, Sophie Topalsky and the Trivanovich Sisters, to mention just a few.

*Top:* The Hegyi Tamburitza Orchestra, 1885-86. Photo courtesy of UCLA Ethnomusicology Dept. *Middle:* Gorica Stanojev Popovich. Photo by Anne Pollock, courtesy of Anne Pollock. *Right:* Vaso Crljenica surrounded by 19 California beauties, 1943. Photo courtesy of Steve Crljenica.

Gorica Stanojev Popovich (above) was born in Lebanon, PA in 1919. She was best known for her recordings with the Croatian orchestra, Veseli Seljaci — whose director, Steve Crljenica, was Gorica's brother-in-law. With Seljaci, Gorica recorded Kazi Cigane, *Uzmi srce moje*, and *Oj cobane*. Serious collectors seek out Gorica's classic *Ancice*, abd Tango of Roses.

When Gorica was sixteen she entered an amateur contest in which the prize was a half-hour segment on WJBK Radio in Detroit. The program consisted of a full orchestra, Gorica's singing and the jokes of Amos Jacobs, who became known to American audiences as Danny Thomas. Rosemarie Mantell, who also sang on the program, became Mrs. Danny Thomas.

In Detroit, before the Second World War, Edo Lubich gave a concert at the Detroit Museum of Art—where he invited Gorica to perform. She sang a few solo numbers and several duets with Edo that received wide public acclaim. Gorica moved to California in 1944 and, although she never recorded with Ivan Konjik, she made many appearances with him accompanied by the Crljenica Brothers. They appeared in San Diego, the Roger Young Auditorium in Los Angeles and Serbian events throughout the West. Gorica was also the alto soloist with St. Steven's Serbian Orthodox Cathedral Choir, and she is remembered for her moving rendition of the Creed she sang during Liturgy for many years.

The 1960s brought a fresh crop of female talent like JoAnn Orlich, Donna Tarailo, Dorothy Mrkelja, Yvonne Spann, Olga Mijhajlovich, Ann Milovanovich, Dawn Stepanovich Kristic and Nancy Vitkovich. Serbian singers always seemed to have 3 essential qualities—beauty, talent and superb singing voices.

Darleen Licina Tubbs of Pittsburgh is one of those individuals. In addition to formal music training, she was introduced to tamburitza singing by Danny Kukich. Her first album was Milo srce ljubav je sve. Since then she has produced 2 tapes—Steve and Darleen and Neighbors and Friends with Steve Zegar. Darleen Licina's parents, Rade and Mary, were first generation Americans who enjoyed music—the Big Band Sound, Broadway tunes, and especially Serbian folk music. They encouraged Darleen's early interest in Serbian singing. Both Darleen and her sister Pam were provided with transistor radios—which were the rage "way back then." Darleen's headphones even accompanied her to bed at night. In the early 60s, as difficult as the economy was, Darleen's parents found a way to finance formal voice lessons and training—which Darleen continued into her college years.

*Top:* Violet Panajatovich Bundalo with the Eli Gruber Tamburitza Orchestra, Milwaukee. Photo courtesy of The Serb National Federation.
*Right:* Serbian Tamburiza Society, "Cica Ilija," Wilmerding, PA, 1932. Standing, Buckie Zivkovich, Miso Blagovich and George Vujic. Seated, Dragi Zivkovich and Sam Blagovich. Photo courtesy of Mila Miller.

*Above:* The Tamburitzans—Evica Rapaich, Bob Jokola, Pete Jokola and Eli Rapiach, 1966. Photo courtesy of Evica Rapaich.

Darleen encourages the junior choir in her church and is heartened by their singing—just as she is equally thrilled to hear Pavarotti. Darleen cannot imagine life without singing. Typical of her modesty, she says: "That it gives enjoyment to others continues to amaze me." We are blessed by her contribution to Serbian music.

California is equally blessed with its share of talent, beauty and voice, with Lisa Milena Simikic who adds a fourth dimension. She is also a talented musician, proficient on the guitar, piano, tambura, violin and conductor. She is currently the director of St. Steven's Serbian Orthodox Cathedral Choir in Alhambra, California. Lisa has performed on television, live radio and in hundreds of concerts. She received her advanced degree at Cal State Northridge, continuing her education at the Wisconsin Conservatory. She performed as soloist with the Milwaukee Symphony Orchestra and the Florentine Opera Company, singing the operas Turandot, Carmen, Manon Lescaut and Faust. Lisa sang at the opening and closing ceremonies of the Olympic Games in Los Angeles in 1984, including a performance at the Hollywood Bowl as part of the Olympic Arts Festival. Lisa is proficient on the guitar, piano, tambura, violin and conducting.

Another talented woman with Pennsylvania roots is Evica Jakola Rapaich (above right), who had established a name for herself in Greensburg, in a group known as Hank Carol and the Carol Sisters, a country music group that appeared on radio, stage and in theaters throughout the East. After moving to California in the mid-1950s, Evica and her brothers Bob and Pete formed the Orao Tamburitzans with fellow musicians Eli Rapaich and Vjekoslav Knezevic. Evica and Eli eventually married; "Knez" departed and the name was changed to The Tamburitzans. The orchestra was active into the 1970s. A highlight of their career was in the 1960s in Lake Tahoe, Nevada, on their first appearance in the Nevada show circuit when they were featured in the top billing with the internationally famous "Viva Le Girls" show from Paris, France. Later in their career, The Tamburitzans opened and operated a show lounge in Downey, California—which was the largest lounge in the Los Angeles area, with a seating capacity of 450. In prior years, The Tamburitzans played at Cigo's Restaurant and Bar in San Pedro, a favorite weekend spot for Southern California Serbs. Pete Jokola is now living in Texas and performing under the name R. C. Taylor. He was selected by the Country Western Music Association of Texas as the "Male Vocalist of the Year" in 1994 and "International Artist of the Year" in 1995. His CD entitled Take Me Back won high ratings in

*Top:* The Hajduk Orchestra, 1965. *Top Row:* Adele Raddish Chadwick, William Dorich, vocalist, Charles Kczman. *Middle Row:* Milan Bosrock, Ted Raddish. *Front Row:* Michael Tomaiko and Dragutin Mijatovich.
*Right:* Opera star, Danica Ilich, soprano, Cincinnati, Ohio. Photo courtesy of The Serb National Federation.

Scandinavia and throughout Europe. His new Gospel release is being well received throughout the Southern United States.

In tambura music men do not even have a corner on slapping a bass, as Micki Likich proved. Velma (Snookie) Milosevich even gave Bob Samazich a run for his money when it came to playing the prima. On page 88, Mladi Becari, popular in Southern California from 1952-78, delighted audiences at every major event throughout the West Coast. In 1957 the group appeared on the television program "Rocket to Stardom," winning first place honors. For several years, Mladi Becari played at the Adriatic Restaurant in Beverly Hills and at The Balkan House in Burbank. They also made regular appearances at Knott's Berry Farm in Anaheim. In 1963, while playing background music at the Bel Air Hotel for a banquet held in honor of King Peter II of Yugoslavia, Mladi Becari invented the *Flaming Pineapple March*, composing it on the spot.

Adele Raddish Chadwick of the orchestra The Hajduk (above) played a mean bass, too, and proved that music runs in many Serbian families. Her father, Ted Raddish, played the cello in the same orchestra and her sister Barbara played the accordion. The Hajduk began in 1950. From 1962 to 1965 the orchestra provided the musical accompaniment for the Aman Folk Ensemble at UCLA (p. 104)—in which I was a dancer and tenor soloist. Shortly thereafter, I became The Hajduk's vocalist. Aman and The Hajduk appeared at the Greek Theater, the Dorothy Chandler Pavilion and in many other public appearances during this period. They also performed in the film *What Did You Do In The War, Daddy?*, produced by Universal Studios. The Hajduk celebrates their 48th year in 1998. They are the longest surviving tamburitza orchestra in California, where they continue to provide Serbian music for many occasions. I, sadly, left the orchestra in 1968 to concentrate on my demanding career. I modestly call myself a musician, too, having played the accordion for 15 years. At the age of 4, I—along with my brother Sam, age 5—formed the youngest accordion and singing duet in Morgantown, West Virginia, appearing on local radio programs and in amateur contests, winning many first place honors—not for our musical talent but for our pint-sized Serbian tenacity. I continued to play accordion and other instruments into adulthood.

Another women's group started during the Second World War in Milwaukee, it was called Kosovo. Their theme song was the *Kosovo Waltz*. The American Srbobran dubbed them "Kosovke devojke" (Kosovo Maidens). Nancy Covis came up with the idea of an all-girl orchestra

*Left:* Darleen Licina Tubbs, Pittsburgh, PA. *Middle:* Jadran Orchestra, Gary, IN. *Right:* Danilo Kozarski, Chicago, IL. Photos courtesy of The Serb National Federation.

in an attempt to keep Serbian music active in Milwaukee during WWII. In July, 1942, she solicited the help of Dorothy Ingich to initiate the task—considering that half of the 8-girl orchestra could not read music. Jack Yelich, an accomplished musician who had played with several orchestras, came to the rescue—he wrote the music in 8 parts and then proceeded to teach them how to read it. In the beginning, having raw fingers and building calluses was beyond the endurance of some. But, surprisingly, their positions were filled immediately. Another obstacle fell in their way—it was necessary for the group to audition before the Milwaukee Musicians' Union Board to obtain membership. During the audition, they were interrupted from their Serbian repertoire and asked "What kind of music is this?" After explaining their Serbian heritage, the Union Board had them play many selections—not because it was necessary—but because they really enjoyed the music. The Kosovo Orchestra was proud to display the banner "American Federation of Musicians—Milwaukee Chapter" everywhere they played, including Pittsburgh, Chicago, South Bend, and Hibbing. After the end of the war, Amelia Radjenovich and Helen Damjanovich retired from the group. When Helen (Obradovich) Basich resigned, Mitzi Sarenac took her place, but staying together became impossible—as marriage, raising families and putting lives back together after the war became more important. On May 25th, 1947, they were down to 5 members: Dorothy Ingich, Mitzi Sarenac, Mileva Pavich, Ann Obradovich and Mileva Borkovich—it was their farewell concert. In the ensuing years the girls have remained close friends. Mileva (Borkovich) Susnar lives in Montecito California, and contributed valuable information and photographs to this article. Amelia (Radjenovich) Bratkovic, June (Jakovich) Crnojevich and Mileva (Pavich) Hosek still live in Milwaukee. Ann (Obradovich) Pavich has the best of both worlds by spending half of the year in Florida and the other half in Milwaukee. Helen (Obradovich) Basich lives in Seminole, Florida.

The old adage "The family that prays together, stays together," could surely be revised to include "playing together," and the Trivanovich family proved as rare a family as the Popovich Brothers. Out of 9 children, 6 would become musicians. Bob and Ned Trivanovich, along with Andy and Nick Kosovich, formed the popular Plavi Jadran Orchestra (Blue Adriatic); while the sisters, Angie, Honey, Mickey and Vi, created the equally popular Trivanovich Sisters Orchestra. What they gave to the people of the Cleveland area from the 1940s to the 1960s is fondly remembered. Honey Trivanovich Zimmerman had 10 children and played tambura while pregnant with 5 of them. After giving birth to the last baby, her nurse in the delivery room

*Left:* Edo Lubich, 1940s. Photo courtesy of Nikki Lubich. *Middle:* Petar Perunovich, 1932. Photo courtesy of Mila Miller. Perunovich returned to Yugoslavia to fight in WWII, during which he died.
*Right:* Jakovac Orchestra, St. Louis, 1940s. Photo courtesy of The Serb Federation.

told Honey: "I have no idea what you were singing during the delivery, but it sure was pretty." The sisters' act included skits and mini plays that kept their audiences laughing. Honey has not lost her touch in this area, as interviewing her for this article was thoroughly entertaining. Some of her colorful comments, unfortunately, could not be put in print. The Trivanovich Sisters played Sremski style instruments, allowing them more intricate fingering while being more pleasurable for them to play. The inevitable consequence of possessing beauty, grace and talent led to marriage and the musical careers of the sisters soon ended. There are now 36 children and at last count 38 grandchildren as of this writing, many of whom are carrying on the Trivanovich music tradition. In 1990, the first video of a tambura group in the United States was made of the Trivanovich Sisters.

The Krajina created many talented musicians, but no family of musicians has achieved more world recognition than the Crljenica Brothers, beginning with Jovo Crljenica—who was born in Kinjacka, near Karlovac, in 1875. Jovo married Mara Dobrijevic in 1900 and came to America in 1903 arriving with 6 tambura instruments under his arms. In 1911 he sent for his wife Mara and sons George and Vaso. By 1910, Jovo moved to Gary, Indiana and began his first 4-piece tamburitza group with family members Ivan, Mile and Milka Stefanac.

In 1913 Jovo's brothers Paul and Lazo came to America. It was at this time that he changed the Farkas system to the Sremski system. His new orchestra was then called Balkan and it included his sons George and Vaso, Velko Savich and Sandor Drakulich. Jovo also organized another orchestra in 1916 with his 2 sons and the Hegyi Brothers. In the early 1920s son George showed exceptional talent on the violin and was sent to New York to study with Professor Ottobar Sevcik. About this time, George was diagnosed with a terminal illness and subsequently died. It was following this tragedy that the family moved to California. Over the ensuing years the Crljenica Brothers, were influential in creating orchestras, teaching music, and entertaining at local Serbian and Croatian events. But the crucial break in the motion picture industry came in 1935, when the Crljenica Orchestra was asked to play for the film *Storm at Daybreak*. Following that, they were engaged to do the sound track to the *Merry Widow*, starring Maurice Chevalier—even appearing in one scene. Paul, who was too young to be out of school, attended classes on the set. Two of the starlets in his classes were Jean Parker and Ann Baxter. In 1938 came the film *The Cat People*, with Fred Astaire and Paulette Goddard. In *Second Chorus* Vaso played *"Shining Moon"* on the prima as Fred Astaire danced. Then came *At the Balalaika* and *The Chocolate Soldier*, with Nelson Eddy and Illona

*Top Left:* Tillie Klaich and The Balkan Serenaders, Steve Vranjes, Nick *"Tillie"* Klaich, Charles Vukovich, seated, Vlad Popovich. *Below Left:* Tillie Klaich. Photos courtesy of Vlad Popovich. *Middle:* George Crljenica, 1922. While studying music under Maestro Ottokar Sevcik, George played in the Chicago Pitt Theater Orchestra at this young age. *Top Right:* Jovo Crljenica with sons Pavle on the left and Steve on the right, Los Angeles, 1936. Crljenica photos courtesy of Steve Crljenica.

Massey, followed by *Taras Bulba* with Yul Brynner and Tony Curtis, then *Ride the Crooked Mile* and *Lawrence of Arabia.* Paul appeared with Bob Hope in *You Got Me Covered,* and Vaso provided the musical accompaniment to Bob Hope in *Road to Morocco.*

It was about this time that Srpski Seljaci Orchestra was organized with Vaso teaching the group. Tambura classes flourished in Los Angeles during this period. Vaso also changed his name to Vasil to satisfy the Russian group he was playing with at the time. Then the family orchestra name was changed to The Crljenica Brothers—Continental Five. In 1940 the orchestra made 3 records on the "Music City" label. A decade later, Music City became Capitol Records.

In 1950, the Crljenica Brothers recorded Steve's composition *"Tamburitza Boogie,"* which sold over a quarter million copies. In the mid-1960s Micha (Mike) Dvorak obtained a permanent position in the Music Department at Walt Disney Studios. Later, Steve joined him there. At Disney, Steve composed *Where Dreamers Go* and *Throughout the Night.* Another milestone came in 1967 when the Crljenica Brothers were asked to do the sound track for *Dr. Zhivago,* the film with Omar Sharif and Julie Christie. At the beginning of the film, immediately after the funeral scene when the young boy looks above his bed at a balalaika, the solo introduction is played by Vasil Crljenica. Tambura music was heard by millions of people throughout the world due to the success of this film. Steve played with the army band featured in one of the scenes in the movie Patton. In the 1960s and 70s the Crljenica boys played occasionally at The Balkan House, a Serbian restaurant in "beautiful downtown Burbank." The restaurant was across the street from the NBC Burbank Studios, where the Johnny Carson Show was taped, very near the Disney Studios and not far from the Universal Studios. The restaurant was owned by Dusan Gagrica and many industry celebrities were regular patrons. Every Saturday night, accordionist Sveta Marich played there during the 1950s-70s.

During this period, Steve's eldest daughter, Linda, joined the group followed shortly thereafter by Steve's youngest daughter Stephanie. They made 3 albums on CB records at the time. Linda Crljenica Regan now teaches in the Garden Grove School District and Stephanie Crljenica Carter teaches in the Irvine School District, after spending 6 years with the Long Beach Symphony. Mitch Dvorak also known as Mike, played with the Seattle Symphony, the Glendale Symphony and the Santa Monica Symphony. Both he and his wife Ann retired from the Disney organization in 1983.

*Far Left:* Mladi Becari Orchestra, 1955-75. *Back Row,* Velma (Snookie) Milosevich, Bob Samarzich, Micki Likich. *Front Row,* Bob Likich and Pete Gaspich. Photo courtesy of Bob Samarzich. *Above:* Angelina Vlajkovich, a popular singer in the U. S. With her is Rasha Radenkovich, an attorney and popular baritone on Belgrade Radio prior to WW II—before he emigrated to the U.S. Photos courtesy of The Serb National Federation. *Right:* Pete Markovich, Milwaukee. Photo courtesy of Helen Popovich.

"Tillie" Klaich of Lackawanna, New York, is fondly remembered by his loyal fans and respected by his fellow musicians. Tillie's heart was bigger than life, and his fondness for children and his desire for them to learn tambura was a driving force in his life. Even as young as 19 years of age, he tackled the challenge of forming a youth group called Veselo Srce, appropriately named (Happy Heart), as that was what Tillie was to his friends. The Balkan Serenaders shared the spotlight with such great entertainers as Vinka and Angelina at the International Cafe. The Serenaders started with Pete Milosevich, Stanko Djuvich, Danny Cugalj, Steve Vranjes and Tillie.

In later years Steve Vranjes was an old standby when Charles Vukovich and Vlad Popovich joined the group. Tillie Klaich and The Balkan Serenaders produced 4 albums which are cherished today; they include: A Continental Toast, Continentally Yours, Sve nase and Cabaret and are included in the Library of Congress archives, where future generations will learn about Serbian showmanship and musical talent. At a private reception, The Balkan Serenaders played at Niagara Falls, Ontario, for the Canadian prime minister and his Serbian wife—Mila Mulroney, who sang a few Serbian songs. They also performed at the Lancaster Opera House and the Buffalo Historical Society and the Festival of American Folklife in Lancaster, New York.

During the Depression, Steve Pavlekovich returned to Bjelovar, Yugoslavia with his mother—where they stayed for over a year. Steve, at the age of 10, was given his first Farkas bisenica—which he mastered so expertly that he began playing with adult musicians. In Bjelovar he learned to play the brac and the violin and played with the orchestra Veselo Drustvo. A year later he returned to Youngstown, Ohio, where he played with George Skrbina—who also selected Matte Vinkovich, Peter Vlajkovich and Dave Zupkovich to form the orchestra Troubadours. After moving to Cleveland, Steve joined forces with Djoko Dokich, John Halik, Mirko Kolesar, Pete Perez and Joe Skornjak. They played for the Cleveland Great Lakes Exposition. At the time, Detroit was a center of tamburitza activity and the entire group decided to move to Detroit. After a few of the musicians decided to return to Youngstown, Steve formed another outstanding group which played for 6 years at the Blue Danube Inn—accompanying such vocalists as Edo Lubich and Vinka Ellesin. The group consisted of Andrija Culig, Leo Baich, Jim Kovachevich and Blaz Tkalac. The Second World War interrupted their musical careers, including Steve's. In the early 1950s Vinka and Steve Pavlekovich produced 2 outstanding albums with musicians John Aberlich,

Top Left: Lira Orchestra, Detroit. Photo courtesy of The Serb National Federation. Left: Voice of America broadcast, 1943. Tambura group not identified. Photo courtesy of Mila Miller. Right: Danny Kukich Orchestra. Walter Naglich, Bill Cvetnic, John Golach and Danny Kukich. Photo courtesy of Danny Kukich.

Tony Burich, Lawrence Mavretich and Blaz Tkalac.

Steve Pavlekovich was instrumental in creating the Detroit Star Junior Tamburitzans (1979-83), the Serbian Junior Tamburitzans (1980-84) and the Serbian Singing Society Ravanica's 50th Anniversary Concert. Following this success, Steve formed the Prijateljski Tambura Zbor—joining Serbs and Croatians of Detroit into one of the finest string orchestras in the area. Steve will be remembered for his dedication to both Serbian and Croatian children who became accomplished musicians.

If Dave Zupkovich never existed, certainly he was the kind of legend that the Serbs would surely have invented. Robust, Dave was bigger than life at over 6 feet, and his orchestra wore bolero-style silk shirts with puffed sleeves. The letter "Z," made of sequins and intricate embroidery, decorated the sashes worn around their waists. The Dave Zupkovich Orchestra included John Krilcich, Tony Markulin and Joe Matacic. They made their mark at Nick and Tony Svetich's Casino Club in Gary, Indiana. Dave was born in Campbell, Ohio. His brother George, nicknamed "Blimp," occasionally sang with the orchestra. George lived in California and had minor roles in motion pictures. Dave played bugarija, violin, banjo, guitar and even percussion instruments. His idol was the French Gypsy guitarist Django Reinhardt. While serving during WWII, Dave was in France and visited The Hot Club many times to listen to Reinhardt, who died in his early 40s. Dave was quite innovative and the Western singer Patsy Cline recorded *Have You Ever Been Lonely?* which became *Je si l' ikad bila tuzna?* From the spin-off of *Te tvoje carne oci* came *Charm of Your Beautiful Dark Eyes* when sung in English. Dave's whistling ability was put to good use in *The Whistler's Polka*. Dave's wife was the former Mildred Vukich, and Dave recorded *Milkina kuca* (Mildred's House) because their house was a way station for every musician in the area. Dave, like Reinhardt whom he admired, died young, too—he was 43. Uros Mamula, musician and Dave's best man at his wedding, received Dave's instrument following his death.

Edo Lubich, one of this century's great musicians, was born in 1912 in Donji Vakuf near Sarajevo. He was a skilled performer who recorded dozens of records on the RCA Victor, Columbia, Decca, Balkan International and Sonart labels. Most people did not know that Edo Lubich was a Bosnian Roman Catholic, because he emphatically called himself a "Yugoslav." He performed with every major Serbian orchestra and performer. For those who were homesick for Yugoslavia after the Second World War, Edo Lubich was a kind

*Top Left:* Tamburashki Zbor "Sloboda," St. Louis, MO, 1930. *Bottom Left:* Angelina Vlajkovich. *Middle:* Militza Kosancich, an opera star in the 40s. Photos courtesy of Serb National Federation. *Bottom Right:* Srpsko Tamburasko Drustvo (1912) was the predecessor of "Banat." Shown are—Zdravko Yezdimir, Lesta Stojanov, Bogdan Kuzmanovich, seated, Vaso and Mirko Bukvich. Photo courtesy of Angie Trbovich.

of touchstone for Yugoslavs in the diaspora. Lubich performed at such fashionable hotels as The Beverly Hills Hotel, The Shamrock in Houston and The St. Regis in New York. His achievements in motion pictures and the number of recordings he made are unmatched—like his recording of Oj, Kaduno with the Verni Orchestra. Lubich also wrote *Cigani mi tvoju, Ja sam majko cura fina, Kukavica Waltz, Ej lolo moja* and *Ja sam Jovicu* with piano arrangements by Slavco Hlad.

Before coming to the United States, Edo Lubich studied in France and received a degree in electrical engineering. He was a versatile singer, adept in 10 languages. A regular on Belgrade Radio, he was popular with his fans in Yugoslavia. Soon his stardom propelled a tour of Paris, Budapest, Rome and Berlin. Edo appeared on German television—being the first Yugoslav to ever appear on television in that country. Edo also appeared in the first sound motion picture made in Yugoslavia and he is mentioned in Europe's motion picture archives. As a graduate of Cornell University and a gourmet, his serious interest in culinary arts was utilized in his later years by opening two upscale restaurants adjacent to Beverly Hills in Century City. The first was called "La Place." But loyal customers began to be confused when Edo opened his second restaurant. In his usual good sense of humor, Edo renamed the second restaurant "Edo's Other Place." It was next door to 20th Century Fox Studios and was frequented by many motion picture stars, such as Greer Garson and Mickey Rooney. Edo sold the restaurants in 1978 and retired in Palm Springs. His 29 year marriage ended when his wife Theresa Yagrik (Hungarian), died in 1974. Edo never remarried and he died in 1993. He is survived by his daughter, Nikki Lubich who lives in Los Angeles, and is following her father's devotion to fine cuisine as a caterer there. His granddaughter, Victoria Federico, lives in the San Francisco Bay Area and holds degrees in Forensic Anthropology and Social Psychology.

Sveta Marich was one of those musicians to accompany Edo Lubich, Vinka, Gorica Popovich and many Serbian singers. At the Balkan House in Burbank, California, Sveta entertained Los Angeles Serbs for 2 decades. He is originally from Cacak, in the heart of Serbia and is known for his rich variety of folk songs and dances. He is no doubt one of the most talented accordionists to come from Yugoslavia. Sveta Marich has been acclaimed as an outstanding virtuoso of the accordion and as an interpreter of Yugoslav folk songs, in addition to songs from Spain, France, Italy and Greece.

*Left:* Sveta Marich, Chicago, 1940s. Photo courtesy of Miloj Ilich. *Center Bottom:* The original Victory Tamburitza, 1942, which became the Plavi Mjesec. George Saula, Ozzie Cavada, Johnny Pribanic, Dusan Saula. Photo courtesy of Ted Phillips. *Center Top:* The Plavi Mjesec in 1983. *Back Row*, Ed Milovac, Sam Saula, Stevan Zegar. Front Row, Danny Kukich, Mark Phillips, Dusan Saula. The Plavi Mjesec continues today with Dusan Saula and his son Mark Phillips. Dusan has been in the St. Nicholas Choir in Monroeville for 50 years, as the director for more than 30. Photos courtesy of Ted Phillips. *Above:* Mia Novich, soprano, popular in the 1960s. Photo courtesy of The Serb National Federation.

The Rankin Bridge was famous for taking people to Kennywood Park. But Rankin, Pennsylvania is most famous for giving us Danny Kukich in 1919. Celebrating more than 60 years as a tambura musician, Danny Kukich and his talented daughter Martha make Pittsburgh Serbs very proud. Danny Kukich started his musical education at the age of 14 with guitar lessons at the Wurlitzer Private School of Music in Pittsburgh. Under the expert training of Max Adkins, Danny learned music theory, harmony, arranging and counterpoint. In the mid-1930s Danny became a member of the Stanley Theater Stage Orchestra as their featured guitarist. He also accompanied various artists and stars performing weekly at the theater in minstrel and vaudeville shows. In 1938 Danny rejected an offer to travel nationally with several major orchestras and elected instead to stay in Pittsburgh and dedicate himself to more tambura music, a decision for which many Serbs remain eternally grateful. He has inspired children and adults for years through his music teaching and coaching as well as composing and arranging. He is called "Maestro Kukich" for a very good reason.

After years of continuous entertaining originally as the Slav Continentals, the orchestra became known as Danny Kukich and His Orchestra. In 1954, Danny accompanied Edo Lubich on the radio program Balkan Gaieties with Charlene Naglich. Danny's career is not limited to the Serbian world. Several jazz artists were fascinated with the tambura sound, and—along with his good friend, Joe Negri, Pittsburgh's number one jazz guitarist and television personality—he recorded many brac and guitar duets. His musical abilities even led to a brief stint playing second violin with the Wilkinsburg Symphony Orchestra. He was also the man behind the music column "Song of the Week" in The American Srbobran, later renamed "Song Corner." Danny was also responsible for training and managing the Avala Tambura Orchestra of Pittsburgh—whose leader was Robert Rade Stone, the president of the Serb National Federation until his recent death. Danny was also one of the members of the popular orchestra, Plavi Mjesec of Monroeville, where he played prima (shown above). A graduate of Carnegie Tech, where he studied printing, Danny worked for 30 years as a printer for The American Srbobran. Danny was named Man of The Year in 1990 by the SNF.. At the beginning of the current civil war in the Balkans, he and Alex Malich collaborated in producing the tape entitled "Mi smo stobom Krajina," and—typical of Alex and Danny—the proceeds went to the Serbian Relief Fund. No one has ever accused Serbian musicians of a lack of charity. All of them, like Danny Kukich, have been more than generous with their talents!

*Top Left:* Crljenica Brothers—Continental Five, recording at Music City, 1933. Vasil, Mitch Dvorak, Steve and Paul behind the unidentified singing artist. *Left:* Jovo Crljenica, 1945. Photos courtesy of Steve Crljenica. *Above:* Continental Strings Tamburitza, 1961. Alex Machaskee, Albert Incorvaia, Bob Arlow and Albert Arlow. Alex Machaskee is the founding member of the Tamburitza Association of America and has served as the chairperson for the Tamburitza Extravaganza over the years. Photo courtesy of The Serb National Federation.

In 1963, Danny Kukich formed the St. Nicholas Serbian Orthodox Jr. Tamburitzans of Wilmerding, organized as a youth cultural organization for the Sunday School members of the St. Nicholas parish. Along with Danny Kukich other talented people are also responsible for this outstanding group: Ron Rendulic who went on to a key position with the Duquesne Tamburitzans, Don Knezevich, Dan Shebetich, Bill Yurkovac and Randy Lugares. Over the years the choreographers included Gerry Bossar, Sharon Boziesvic, Erin George, Millicent Novak, Linda Metala, Jack Poloka, Mary Agnes Posatko, Marilyn Puscarich, Kathy Rendulic, Carla Tozzi, Donna Vranesevic, Debra Vucelich, Denise Vukic, Susan Williams and Michaelann Yurkovac.

Former governor of Pennsylvania, Richard Thornburgh, invited the St. Nicholas Tamburitzans to represent the Serbian community in a program called "Christmas an Ethnic Experience." The group's longevity of some 30 years is a testimony to the Serbs of Monroeville, the dedication of the staff and the commitment of these parents.

Martha Kukic is a musician in her own right, beginning her music career at the age of 7 under the wing of her father, Danny. Martha grew up with a violin in one hand and a Barbie Doll in the other. At the age of 10, Martha became a member of the Pittsburgh Youth Symphony and the Wilkinsburg Junior Symphony and was featured as a violin soloist in both orchestras. She attended the Duquesne University School of Music and holds a Bachelor of Science and Master's Degree in Music Education. Martha Kukic is the director of the Holy Trinity Cathedral Choir of Pittsburgh and the musical instructor of her own church choir, St. Nicholas, of Monroeville.

The previously mentioned Plavi Mjesec of Monroeville, got its start in 1941 when John Pribanich found himself in front of the Rantovich Tavern in Trafford after an exhausting streetcar ride from Masontown. John left his family to seek work in Trafford, but, instead, founded the Victory Tamburitza—which was changed to Plavi Mjesec (Blue Moon) in 1942. In addition to John Pribanich, that first orchestra included Arthur Drakulic, Mel Paich, Ed Milovac and Mike Gotich. But the war brought instant changes—and Ed Milovac was replaced by George Saula. Gradually, all the members left for Europe or the South Pacific. In 1946 the orchestra was again reorganized to include Tom Kukich and Dusan and Sam Saula.

East Pittsburgh Serbs remember the evenings spent listening to Plavi Mjesec at Marion's Tavern in Large,

*Left:* Angie, Honey, Mickey and Vi Trivanovich. Photo courtesy of Honey Trivanovich Zimmermann. *Above:* Hegyi Brothers, Edward and John, with Theresa Hegyi seated in the middle, 1898. (Bass player unknown). Photo courtesy of Duquesne University. *Above Right:* Desanti, an opera singer, 1940s. *Bottom Right:* Vasil and George Crljenica, 1913. Photos courtesy of The Serb National Federation.

PA, Dan's Bar in McKeesport, the Serbian Club in Duquesne, the Arlington Inn, Clairton's Columbia Hotel and, of course, Vinka Ellesin's Selo Inn. Every Saturday was spent on WLOA Radio in Pittsburgh.

Omaha, Nebraska was the birthplace of the great orchestra Tamburitza Zbor "Soko," formed in 1927. The Orchestra became one of the best string orchestras in the United States. The first teacher of this group was George Kachar, a dedicated musician and teacher who taught many of the young musicians of this century— including the Popovich Brothers. One of those first classes was in Walsenburg, Colorado in 1921. Soko played in Serbian colonies in Kansas City, St. Louis, St. Paul, Duluth, Chisholm and Des Moines. They also played at Radio Station WOWT, where Johnny Carson got his start. In 1929, George Kachar was replaced in Soko by Frank Buckingham, professor of music at the University of Omaha. George went on to form Tamburitza Zbor, Peoria, Illinois in 1933, Tamburitza Zbor "Yugoslavia," in Gary, Indiana, in 1934 and Kachar's Orchestra Club Zbor in Gary, Indiana, in 1937. He played in each of these groups. George Kachar was not just a teacher and conductor, he composed music and insisted that his pupils learn to read music. Kachar arrived in the United States at the age of 14. Just 5 years later, in 1921, George was teaching and writing music. His son,

Del Kachar, who goes by the name Casher, says there is literally no explanation for his father's expertise in music. One thing is apparent—many Serbian musicians in the 1930s and 40s have George Kachar to thank for having the foresight to pass on his genius.

The name Soko came from the Czechs. In 1909, Milan Zemunski came to Omaha with his grandfather. In those days there were no Serbian churches or social clubs. The local Czechs took the Serbs under their wing and a Soko group was formed. It was successful until WWI broke out and many of these emigrant Serbs volunteered to go back to Serbia and fight in the war. Losing all those young men, Milan Zemunski decided to start another Soko group, this time with young boys. In 1926 Milan asked the Sokoli if he could form a tamburitza orchestra and they took the name Soko. That original group included Eli Drakulich, Joe Churchich, Mike Churchich, Mike Medakovich and Milan Zemunski. Mike Churchich is the lone survivor.

When music talent is passed from father to son, it is noteworthy—particularly in the case of Del (Kachar) Casher, son of George Kachar, the first teacher of Soko. Del is known in Los Angeles for his musical scores for motion pictures, including the recent film First Knight with Sean Connery. He appeared with Elvis Presley at

*Top Left:* Edo Lubich singing to Greer Garson and Mickey Rooney, 1952. *Above:* Edo Lubich, 1930s. Photos courtesy of Nikki Lubich. *Middle Top:* Crljenica Orchestra, Steve, Mildred, Mary Baich (a cousin) and Vasil and Jovo Crljenica, 1924. Photo courtesy of Steve Crljenica. *Left:* Vasil Crljenica, Frank Kirincic, Jovo Crljenica (unidentified) and George Crljenica, 1918. Photo courtesy of Steve Crljenica.

Paramount Pictures in Roustabout. His background includes producer, arranger and performer for the music in the television series The New Zoo Revue and Chico and the Man. His guest appearances include shows with Bob Hope, Buddy Rogers, Buddy Ebsen, Peggy Lee, Julie London, Bobby Troup, Brenda Lee, Bobby Vinton, Billy Vaughn and guest artist performances for the LA Pops Orchestra and the Orange County Symphony.

When Warren Beatty wanted that certain musical sound for the picture Love Affair, he asked Del to introduce the balalaika in the sound track—but Del Casher convinced him to just listen to a few selections on the tambura. Warren Beatty instantly agreed and Del performed the music for the sound track and also appeared in the film. In the 1960s Del performed with Gene Autry's Melody Ranch television program and the Lawrence Welk Show, examples of his versatility. Del Casher arrived in Hollywood from Hammond, Indiana as a young man of 15. He initiated his Hollywood recording studio by producing a then unknown singer/song writer named Carole King, and he pioneered new ground in guitar sound effects while playing with a young Frank Zappa. He also played with Les Paul, David Rose, Johnny Green and Henry Mancini. As a young man, Del had a reputation among his musical colleagues as "that kid with all the black boxes." His use of a prehistoric delay device called the "echophonic" mystified fans and players alike. Del became one of the first artist endorsees for another pioneer in the music industry—Fender Musical Instruments. Del continues to consult for Fender and has played on nearly every Fender guitar ever made—from the old Jaguar to the new Strat Plus, his current favorite. As president and founder of California Recording, Inc., Digital Post in Burbank, Del continues to participate in sound tracks for motion pictures, much to our enjoyment.

In 1912, in Elizabeth, New Jersey, Zdravko Yezdimir—along with Vaso and Mirko Bukvich, Lesta Stanojev and Bogdan Kuzmanovich—began the Banat Orchestra, which started as Srpsko Tamburasko Drustvo. They played together for 60 years and appeared in such American cities as Philadelphia, Steelton, Lebanon, Baltimore, New York and New Jersey. Newcomers to Banat included such talented musicians as Wally Yezdimir, Eddie Bachinich and Milan Yosich. Accordionists were added to enhance the sound. One of those musicians was Dushan Petrov and, later, Milutin Yezdimir joined in. Substituting from time to time were the brothers Veljko and Djoka Radin.

*Top Left:* The Orao Strings, South Bend, Indiana. T.G. Petrovich was teacher and leader, early 1930s. Photo courtesy of Helen Popovich. *Bottom Left:* Butcher's Club, Detroit, 1940s. Photo courtesy of The Serb National Federation. *Above:* Srpsko Tamburasko Drustvo. Top Row, Izija Alexsich, Dragutin Basich, Mladin Lemunija, Mark Milatovich. Front Row, Dragutin Manitasevich, Vlado Marjanovic and Anjelko Basich, Indianapolis, Indiana, 1900. Photo courtesy of Helen Popovich.

In 1938 one of those unforgettable moments in life could be described when Banat Orchestra was invited to play on the Schooner "Jadran" with Yugoslav Counsel Bozidar Stojanovic. Joined by the Binicki Choir of Lebanon, Pennsylvania, they sang Jadransko Morje and Dalmatinski sajkas, to homesick Serbs. Banat was invited to represent the American Serbs at the opening of the Yugoslav Pavilion at the World's Fair in New York City in 1939. Zdravko and his Banat Orchestra worked with the Herman Folk Dancers in New York for more than 20 years.

One of 6 inductees to the Tamburitza Hall of Fame in 1995 was Lazo Marinovich. He shared the spotlight that year with Michael "Mitch" Dvorak and Alex Machaskee. Lazo spent 62 years in tamburitza music and was teacher and instructor of tamburitza music at Milwaukee's St. Sava Serbian Church. Born in Slovenia in 1908, Marinovich arrived in this country in 1911—settling in Milwaukee with his mother. He began studying tambura under George Tossenberger, his mentor and lifelong friend. Lazo mastered the brac, cello, prim and bass. With Tossenberger, Lazo formed The Continental Strings in the 1930s. Edward Hegyi and Frank Weber were early members. The Continental Strings played at some of the famous restaurants in Milwaukee and became the staff musicians on Radio WEMP in the late 1940s. The Continental Strings toured with Frankie Yankovich, the legendary "Polka King," who died in 1998. They also performed regularly at the Club Paragon in the late 40s and early 50s. Lazo and his family moved to Phoenix in 1966, where he began Orchestra Troubadours—which was popular until 1982. Lazo Marinovich died a few years later.

In the 1920s George and Vaso Crljenica tutored the orchestra Lika, an orchestra that included Dave Durock, George Japa, Milan Mandich, George Mandich and Novica Minich. By the early 1930s a newer version of music was heard in South Bend with the Orao Orchestra, which was organized by Louis Yazich and Walter Medich with Steve Mandich and starring Michael Polovina on the violin. Over the years the group also included Steve Madich, Bob Medich and Fred Madich, Steve's brother, and Orish Pamuchena. They played until the mid 1960s. It took more than 15 years before a third tambura group was to be heard in South Bend. Ronald Balaban and Steve Madich, Jr. brought back to life the music of Steve Madich, Sr. Steve Madich played and built many fine instruments before he died. A bit of public celebrity was added to the new group when Lazo Mihajlovich joined. Sports fans will recall his illustrious football career at Indiana University.

*Top Left:* Soko Orchestra, 1929. Top Row, Mike Churchich, Eli Drakulich, Mike Medakovich, Petar Markovich, Tom Zoroya. Seated, Milan Zemunski, the founder, Tony (?), Professor Frank Buckingham and Joe Churchich. *Bottom Left:* The 1936 new Soko orchestra with Milan Zemunski. Photos courtesy of John Zemunski. *Above:* The Crljenica Orchestra, 1972. Steve, his daughter Stephanie, Vasil, Linda, also Steve's daughter, and Paul. Photo courtesy of Steve Crljenica.

Michael Polovina's ability in musical composition was known in the Orao Orchestra, but few people know that many of his songs are registered by ASCAP and have been published and sung by other artists. These include such titles as *My Lonely Serenade* and *I'll Be Coming Back Your Way*. But those who know him best are his fellow parishioners who enjoyed his service to his church as a pojac (cantor).

For those of us fortunate enough to have visited former Yugoslavia and to have seen the Dunav, or the famous Danube River, the selection of the name Dunav has a special meaning. This foursome of gifted musicians brought honor to the famous river and to themselves, while lavishing their talents on the Serbian communities throughout the Midwest. They made their debut at Nick and Tony's Casino Club in Gary, Indiana and are remembered as one of the great tamburitza groups in America. The lead was Steve Makarevich, whose Russian heritage added a special Slavic sound, as much as the talent of George Halaschak, whose distinct madjar (Hungarian) sound provided great depth to their music. The tenor soloist, Steve Vucinich, can also be heard on early Serbian records by Roko Abramovich, John Krilich and Dave Zupkovich. Their brac players included such talented musicians as George Medakovich, Richard Savage and Martin Kapugi. The newer generations of talent included Frank Jovanovich, John "Bucky" Bukvich and Pete Plecas.

Richard Savage was born in Akron, Ohio in 1924. In a family of 4 sisters and a brother, Richard came by his music talent through his parents. Ljuba (Ruby), his mother, played bass and his father played bugarija. They both spoke 7 languages. "Richie," as he was known to his friends and fans, learned to play the prima from Joca Radic, one of the family's boarders. The first song he learned to play was Srbijanci i Bosanci—and that was at the age of 7. His father took him to Joe Adich's Tavern and sat his son on the bar, where he played his "first" job. If not at Adich's Tavern, they were at the Serbian church in Gary or in East Chicago, Indiana listening to the Popovich Brothers, Edo Lubich, Vinka, the Kapugi Brothers, Djoko and Mel Kokich or other idols of their generation. By 1940 Richard Savage was playing with Slavuj in Whiting, Indiana and Novi Zivot in East Chicago. In 1941, at the request of Joe Skertich, Richard joined the Skertich Brothers Orchestra, a Croatian orchestra. He remained with them for over a dozen years. During this period, Richard composed Frog Valley Polka, Dreamer and Moja zvezdica—which were recorded on the Columbia label. In the 1960s he played with Drina Orchestra and Dunav. In 1976 he joined Banat Orchestra after his open-heart

*Above:* Club Soko Orchestra, Gary, Indiana, 1929. Vasil Crljenica seated on the right with George Kachar seated on the left. Photo courtesy of Del (Kachar) Casher, George's son. *Top Right:* The Balkan Mountain Men, Matt Vucin, Milan Vemi, Frank Toplak, Jim Kovacevic and Ivan Vidak. Photo courtesy of Duquesne University. *Right:* Richard Savage. Photo courtesy of Alex Machaskee. *Far Right*: Mark Phillips, Plavi Mjesec Orchestra, Monroeville, PA. Photo by William Dorich.

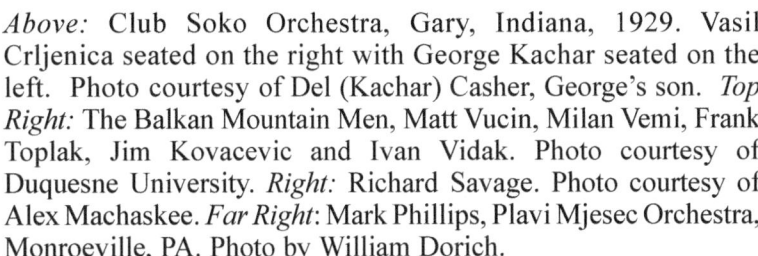

surgery. He was inducted into the Tamburitza Hall of Fame in 1983.

One cannot mention Gary, Indiana without first recognizing Steve Barich, whose heroic war time experience was once described by Milan Opacich in Serb World Magazine as reading like "Tolstoy's War and Peace." I also like to think of Steve Barich as the Serbian Danny Kaye, for his love of children and teaching them the pleasures of playing music. As a teenager, he joined the orchestra Yugoslavija—which was tutored by a young man whose name was Adam Popovich. The Yugoslavija orchestra was quite popular until WWII broke out in 1941, when Steve went off to defend his country. After the war, Steve joined the Balkan Orchestra of Chicago—blending his talents with Milan and Bob Panajatovich and Nick Drobac. In a few years, Steve joined the Zora Orchestra, which enjoyed great success. Still, Steve always found the time to utilize his talents—this time with the 25-piece Tambura Ensemble of South Chicago.

Forever associated with Gary, Indiana and Middle America is The Nite Rose Inn, which still brings a smile to many Serbian faces. In the 1940s one of the popular groups playing there was the Kosovo Orchestra of South Chicago with Nick Babich, Pete Klasnja, Pete Mistovich, Pete Varichak and Eli Potkonjak. Kosovo Orchestra was a spirited group in which Nick Babich was affectionately called "Gloves," for his talented fingers on the prima. When Kosovo dissolved, Nick went on to play cello for Dunav Orchestra and Pete Mistovich replaced Eli Popovich on the berda (bass) when Eli resumed his military career.

Dusan Jovanovich and the Drustvo Orao Tamburitza Orchestra of Philadelphia were known to the Hungarians, Croats, Romanians and the Serbs—all of whom loved his music and claimed him as their own—in spite of the fact that Dusan Jovanovich was a Serb. He recorded more than 75 records on the old Columbia green label. In those early days of the 1920s no matter how meager the means, somehow most families could afford a Victorola. Dusan Jovanovich also recorded for RCA, featuring Romanian dances and folk songs. To the Romanian audience, he was known as Dusan Joanovichu—and he was teamed with George Ivascu, without a doubt a Romanian. These recordings were made in Camden, New Jersey. Dusan was from the Banat border near Romania, explaining why his knowledge of the Romanian language and that of the Hungarians was so proficient. His 1927 recordings included the Hora (Circle Dance) and the Invartita (Swirl Dance), and included a viola and a clarinet. When we remember the RCA

*Above Left:* The original 8 women of the Kosovo Orchestra, which performed in Milwaukee. Back Row, Helen Damjanovich, Dorothy Ingich and Ann Obradovich. Front Row, Amelia Radjenovich, Helen Obradovich, Mileva Pavich, June Jakovich and Mileva Borkovich. *Left:* Poster of the first Kosovo concert at Polonia Hall, 1944. Photos courtesy of Mileva Borkovich Susnar. *Above:* Adam Popovich leads the Sloboda Choir in front of Chicago's Apollo Theatre in 1943 for the opening of the film "*Chetniks.*" Photo courtesy of Mitzi Alexich.

label with the famous dog listening to "his master's voice," we know that he was listening to Dusan Jovanovich. Early collectors also heard the voice of Dusan Jovanovich's wife, who made comic records—popular during this era. The skits or mini plays included such titles as Tako se Zivi u Americi (That's How You Live in America) and Sima kurta-bootlegger (Sam the Bootlegger). Even more popular were the "risque" skits, such as Maksa trazi burt (Max is Looking for a Boarding House), that required sending the children out of the room before playing them. Little is known of Dusan Jovanovich. We know that in 1929 the entire Orao Orchestra was killed in an auto-train accident. We also know that Dusan Jovanovich was one of the most prolific recording Serbian artists of this century. He recorded more than 100 records between 1925 and 1929, setting a recording record that would be the envy of any artist today. Dusan also brought a splendid Serbian sense of humor to America—something they all needed in those days, as we do today.

Jimmy "Zivan" Katich, was a second-generation tambura player, who excelled on the prima and doubled on both brac and cello. Today, his father lives in St. Louis, but Zivan is no longer with us—a loss to tamburitza music and to Serbian-American pride. The famous Sarinian Arch that frames the St. Louis skyline is a tribute to man's architectural and engineering genius. It is also a rainbow that reminds the Serbs of St. Louis that Zivan was here. Zivan's mother, Vera Katich, directed the Holy Trinity Choir in St. Louis for over 50 years. She taught choral directing to Michael Martinovich and Petar Buha, the current choir instructor. Vera received the Serbian Orthodox Choir Association's Honorary Lifetime Members Award in 1980. She is survived by her daughter, Donna Katich, an alto singer in St. Steven's Cathedral Choir in Alhambra, California.

St. Louis, the gateway to the West, is also the home of the great St. Louis Symphony—one of the oldest musical groups in the United States. St. Louis is also an area where prominent Serbs of the period are well known; like Petrovich, Veselinovich, Putich, Tomich, Katich and Misa Boskovich and his tamburaski orchestra Zbor Sloboda, founded in the 1930s. Twenty years later, when the Sloboda Orchestra was revived, familiar names would once again appear in St. Louis tamburitza—Katich, Tomich and Boskovich. Included in that group were Michael Martinovich and George Cavic. Michael Boskovich, grandson of Sloboda founder Misa Boskovich, and son of Harold Boskovich, followed in the family tradition by playing the berda. He now resides in Omaha, where he owns an advertising agency. George Cavic lives in San Francisco, where he is an executive with Parke-Davis Pharmaceuticals—one of this nation's leading

*Top Left:* The Maksimovich Brothers, John, Branko, Ivan and Milan during their performance at the first Serbian Singing Festival in 1936 in Akron, Ohio. Photo courtesy of Branko Maksimovich. *Bottom Left:* Ted Popovich, at a 1972 Testimonial. Photo courtesy of Mitzi Alexich. *Left:* Maksimovich Brothers in a 1937 Los Angeles appearance. Photo from the Los Angeles Times, courtesy of Branko Maksimovich. *Above:* Martha Kukich playing violin with the Danny Kukich Orchestra with John Golach and Walter Naglich. Photo courtesy of Martha Kukich.

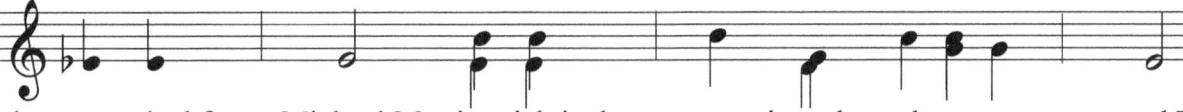

pharmaceutical firms. Michael Martinovich is the son of baseball great, Boris Martinovich. He is an executive with CBS Records in Nashville. Bratso Tomich still resides in St. Louis and is still a lead singer, playing the bugarija.

St. Louis was also the original American home for Vojislav Vasich, known for many years in Yugoslavia for his orchestra, The Montenegro Five. At the age of 14, Voja studied the upright bass violin—becoming so proficient that he became a member of the symphony where he began his early interest in the 6-string guitar, an instrument that he was to master. The Montenegro Five shared the same Liverpool, England manager responsible for the success of the Beatles. Before coming to the United States, Vojan entertained in Germany and his international music was a favorite in Saint-Moritz, Switzerland—where Vojan first played for King Peter II, the exiled Yugoslav monarch. The group was soon booked for appearances in Kiev, St. Petersburg and in the Ukraine and Latvia. The Montenegro Five was also popular in Bratislava, Czechoslovakia and in the Scandinavian cities of Oslo and Stockholm.

In former Yugoslavia, Vojislav Vasich accompanied such great vocalists as the late Zivan Milic, Predrag Gojkovic and Victoria Jovanovic. He was the first artist to have the courage to record Tamo Daleko after the Second World War, much to the consternation of the Tito government. After coming to America, Vojan graduated in mechanical engineering and operated a foreign car repair service in St. Louis for many years. He recorded more than a dozen albums and continued his musical career. He now lives in Chicago.

"Dobro dosli brac Maksimovich" was the headline written by Rad Porubovich, editor and publisher of Domovina (The Fatherland), on March 26, 1937 in the Los Angeles-based newspaper. The Los Angeles Times the same day wrote:"Four Yugoslavian brothers from the University of Belgrade sang at an informal Sunday night party given in their honor in North Hollywood by Mrs. William Powell"—wife of the famous actor. The Maksimovich Brothers (above) completed an 11 country tour before appearing at the first Serbian Singing Festival in Akron, Ohio in 1936. After the SSF concert, the Montenegrin-born brothers went on a tour of the United States receiving standing ovations. In an article in The American Srbobran in June, 1936, Millie Velimirovich wrote: "The Maksimovich Brothers go with their eternal songs pouring life into the starved hearts of the sons and daughters of a race whose very existence depends on music."

*Left:* George Kachar, center, and his orchestra, Tamburitza Zbor, Peoria, Illinois, 1933. Photo courtesy of his son Del Casher. *Middle:* Del (Kachar) Casher and Warren Beatty on the set of *"Love Affair."* Photo courtesy of Del Casher. *Right:* Lisa Milena Simikic, 1987. Photo courtesy of SNF.

Spremte se spremte Cetnici (Prepare, Chetniks, Prepare) recorded by Mirko Markovich and Rash Redenkovich at the beginning of World War II, became the battle cry for freedom-loving Serbs. Mirko and Rasha were classmates at Belgrade University before migrating to America. By the time the war started in 1941, they were well known among the Serbian community. Rasha had his own radio program on NBC before his career took him throughout the United States performing in grand hotels and clubs. Mirko Markovich was self-taught and had a seemingly infinite collection of songs.

Marko Popovich even coined one song as *Markovich's kolo*. Both Mirko and Rasha were guest soloists of past Serbian Singing Festivals. Their legacy of recordings continues to enrich the musical heritage of the Serbian people of this century.

Julius Peskan made his mark on tamburitza music. He also leaves us a living treasure in a made-for-television movie entitled Toma, in which he played his violin in a wedding scene. A Romanian, born in Banat in the town of Torac, Julius studied violin at the Conservatory of Music in Timisora, Rumania. He joined the orchestra Petrovich, better known as "Bocalut," and he also played with renowned violinist Durain of Vladimirovac. In Chicago he played with Sar Planina orchestra and appeared on television in a program called International Cafe. Even famous people were under the spell of Julius' violin. Zsa Zsa Gabor, the Hungarian actress, hired Julius to entertain at some of her celebrated Hollywood parties. Julius played with Martin and Frank Kapugi and Dave Zupkovich and accompanied such great Serbian singers as Angelina. In a one-take recording called Jammin' With Julius, Horace Mamula, Jack Tomlin, Milan Opacich and Julius revealed that anybody can make a record by judicious editing and numerous takes—but Julius proved that talented musicians can excell under pressure. Julius Peskan always associated himself with outstanding artists such as timbalist Ion Carlig, a colleague of the noted violinist and composer, Dinicu, who wrote Hora Stacato—a song made famous by Jasha Heifetz.

When Serbs play classical music, we take great pride in their accomplishments. It is indeed rare however, for a Serb to play a Mozart mandolin solo on a prima—that is history making music. Mike Radicevich played the prima solo with the Florentine Opera Company and played the Vivaldi Concerto for Mandolin as a guest performer for the Milwaukee Civic Orchestra in 1988. This was from 1985-88 when Mike also had his Starigrad Orchestra with Dawn Radicevich on the violin, Jim Waller on the guitar, Mike on brac and prima with Lisa Milena Simikic on the cello and doing

*Left:* Orkestar Mladost, Alhambra, California, 1996. Lisa Milena Simikic, director, with Novica Bozunovich on the prima, Milan Cvejic, accordian, Larissa Kowalyk, bass, Stephen Lovrensky, brac, Meghan McKenna, violin, Victoria Skundrich, prima, Angela Stoyanoff, prima, Elena Vrska, prima, Crystal Warren, prima and Thomas Warren, bugarija. Photo by William Dorich. Above: The Popovich Brothers in 1975. Photo courtesy of Adam Popovich.

the vocals. The late Cyril Seso expertly played the ancient Hungarian instrument, cymbalom, to the delight of their audiences. This unique combination of talent was available to Milwaukee residents on any given night when they were treated to a bit of country, a few show tunes, tambura and a touch of opera. Jim Waller, who accompanied the country western singer Patsy Cline, joined Mike Radicevich in making sure that experiencing Starigrad and the Old Town Restaurant was like stepping into old Belgrade.

In the age-old process of one musician passing on her talents and experience to the next generation Lisa Milena Simikic devoted her spare time for a few years to teach a young group called Orkestar Mladost (above), at St. Steven's Cathedral in Alhambra, California and Slava Orchestra for young beginners. Her efforts and their dedication, once again, prove a winning combination in preserving our Serbian customs and music.

Junior tamburitza groups flourished in the United States in the 1930s and 40s. In the 1950s when everyone in the world was emulating everything in America, including our trends in Rock and Roll, tamburitza music began to dissipate and disappear. In the early 1960s another revival in everything ethnic reappeared, thanks to groups like Aman at UCLA and the rededication of older musicians aware that this music will die unless it is passed on to the young. In 1969 in South Chicago, the Popovich Brothers were again the inspiration in creating the St. Archangel Michael Tamburitzans. Like most groups of 30 or 40 young musicians, only a handful continue to keep music in their lives. But this particular group of youngsters was different, perhaps because of the influence of the Popovich Brothers. Pete and Mike Narancic continued to spark their tamburitza interest. George Ivancevich, now an attorney, is a member of the Jesen Orchestra and always finds the time to play music. Bob Lalich and John Lazich play with the Popovich Brothers Orchestra, while Nick Rakich plays with the Drina Orchestra. Scott Barach, Carl Schutzman, Jr., and John Zevkovich were all members of the Mladi Becari Quartet. The St. Archangel Michael Junior Tamburitza was directed by Martin Kapugi. His assistant was Slavko Lazich.

In San Francisco, in 1981, the juniors organized as the St. John Youth Orchestra. They played until 1985. After these young musicians obtained their educations and established their careers, several of the group formed the Becari Orchestra. Sviraj—the Serbian word meaning to "play" is an appropriate name for this talented group of Balkan musicians. Born in Steelton, Pennsylvania, they grew up as friends and their friendship has created one of the most unique sounds in ethnic music.

*Above:* Sviraj, Balkan Jam, (1996) Danilo Yanich, Lenny Tepsich and Raczar Lopatic, Jr. Photo courtesy of Danilo Yanich. *Right:* The Bajich Brothers, 1996. Bozidar, Vince Rodina, Peter, Front Row, Paul and Borislav. Photo courtesy of the Bajich Brothers.

The Philadelphia Inquirer wrote: "Sviraj plays the bejabbers out of Balkan and East European folk music." Their performances evoke passion, fire, sadness, joy and melancholy. The music has its roots in Serbia, Macedonia, Bosnia, Croatia, Dalmatia and Romania, but it also flourishes among the Balkan communities of North America. Sviraj preserves both traditions because both nurtured them. Sviraj has performed together since 1988 before appreciative audiences at The Library of Congress, The Smithsonian Institution, Disneyworld, Orlando, the Universities of Pennsylvania, Delaware, Carnegie-Mellon and George Mason. They have become a regular at the Tamburitza Association of America's Extravaganzas. They have performed at The Pennsylvania State Museum, the Folklore Society of Greater Washington, the Pennsylvania League of Cities, Philadelphia Folksong Society, Susquehanna Folk Festival, Bethlehem Musikfest, Cherry Tree Music Co-op, and the American Society of Ethnomusicologists. They have performed on folk music radio shows and for events in ethnic communities throughout the United States.

R. E. (Raczar) Lopatic, Jr. who plays violin, prim, and provides vocals for Sviraj is of Slovenian and Croatian descent. He is a former member of the Duquesne Tamburitzans and is a classically trained violinist. Raczar has been performing and teaching for more than 20 years and entertained at Walt Disney World in Florida for several years. He is now back in the Pennsylvania area. Lenny Tepsich plays bass, cello and provides vocals and is of Serbian and Croatian heritage. He, too, has performed for over 20 years. He has been featured at Balkan music and dance camps and international folk festivals. An accomplished tamburitza cello player, he adds the counter-melodies that give the music richness and texture. Also known by thousands of adoring young fans as "Mr. Music," Lenny performs regularly at schools, special education functions and at children's hospitals in the Pennsylvania area. He is a regular performer at Hershey Park. Danilo Yanich plays bugarija and accordion and provides vocals. He is a Serb and has performed for over 25 years. A former music director for the Tomov Folk Dance Ensemble of New York, he is on the teaching staff of Balkan Music and Dance Camps and is past president of the National Board of the East European Folklife Center. He holds a Ph.D. in Urban Affairs and Public Policy, and in addition to teaching in that graduate school at the University of Delaware he has published several articles on Balkan issues. The Baltimore Folk Music Society was accurate when they said of Sviraj: "Whether vocal or instrumental, their music immediately touches the soul."

*Above:* Jedinstvo Orchestra, Phoenix, Arizona, 1996. Nick Vudrag, Mike Swagel, Mitch Zakula and Mark Marusich. Photo courtesy of Jedinstvo Orchestra. *Top Right:* Petar Radovich Orchestra, photo courtesy of Radovich Orchestra.

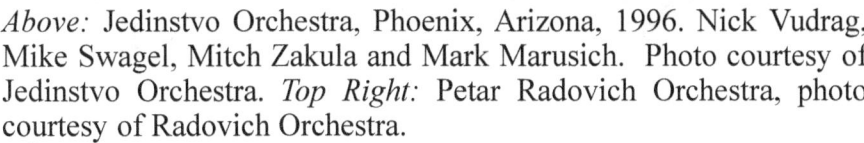

The Bajich Brothers (above) are the sons of a Serbian Orthodox priest, Very Rev. Milan Bajich, and the late Protinica Mary Bajich. Their talent and their love of music was nurtured by a father with a great musical sense of his own and a mother with a lovely and captivating soprano voice. Their 4 sisters, Tijana, Seja, Jelena, Miryana, are also musically talented. It has been said that if The Bajich Brothers were at the Battle of Jericho, Joshua would not have needed trumpets. With the singing and playing of The Bajich Brothers the walls would come tumbling down! All 4 brothers played the violin in school, so it was only natural to transfer their musical training to the instruments of their heritage—the tambura. The eldest brother, Bozidar or Bozhi as he is fondly called, became a member of the Novi tamburitza orchestra in 1973, while 2 younger sisters formed a youth group. During this time the 3 younger brothers, Borislav (Bati) and the twins, Peter and Paul, were being taught by Sam Krajnovich who led them in the Balkan Echoes. Separated by only a year, these 3 grew up more like triplets. After 5 years they joined their older brother Bozhi and the late Vince Rodina in the Novi orchestra.

By 1981, they succumbed to the voices of encouragement of friends and family and formed The Bajich Brothers. Vince Rodina provided the musical support—and he was always there for the brothers as a fellow musician, mentor and friend until his death in 1995. The Bajich Brothers have become known to Serbs throughout North America from St. Petersburg, Florida, to Jackson, California.

The Jedinstvo Orchestra (shown above) was formed in 1984 when Bob Chubrich introduced Mike Swagel and Nick Vudrag to each other, knowing they shared a love of tamburitza music. Neither had played in a tamburitza orchestra, but they were driven by a desire to have an orchestra. By the end of that year, Jedinstvo was formed and the group included Mark Borato on the brac, Mike Swagel on prim, Nick Vudrag on bugaria and +Bob Terzich on bass. Bob was replaced by Mike Swagel's brother Steve, a drummer who quickly learned to play bass. Mitch Zakula, a fine prima player, was added to the group in mid-1986. In 1987, Mark Borato left the group to join Cetri tamburitza orchestra. In 1990, Steve Swagel moved back home to Buffalo, New York, leaving Mike to take over the bass. Jedinstvo suddenly became a trio with occasional support by such cello players as Pete Plechas, who played on the first Jedinstvo recording, George Ivancevich and Walt Naglich. When Mark Marusich became available to take over the bass, Mike Swagel switched back to cello. This is the current configuration of the orchestra. Nick Vudrag grew up

Aman Folk Ensemble, UCLA, 1965, with the Hajduk Orchestra. Photo by William Dorich.

In the early 1960s, when Aman was formed at UCLA, I was astounded to discover this group of 90 students who dedicated themselves to ethnomusicology and the preservation of the music of my heritage. When I joined Aman in 1964, Anthony Shay, a Croatian, was the director of the ensemble. He and I were the only members at the time with Yugoslav heritage. I was flattered that students who were Jewish, Hispanic and Anglo-Saxon Protestants were consumed with preserving the music, dances and costumes of my culture, when most young Serbs in my generation were not. It was the highest form of flattery that some of these students minored in the Serbian language and spoke the tongue of my ancestors. Our fathers and grandfathers wanted us to be good Americans, however, I am confident that they never intended that our assimilation into the American culture required the abandonment of our rich ethnic roots. The musicians in this story have proven that we can preserve both.

This is not the end—but merely the beginning of another century of Serbian music.

*Top Photo:* George Kachar's Zbor Orchestra, Gary, Indiana, 1934. Photo courtesy of Del Casher. *Top Right:* Nicholas Vasich with the famous violinist, David Rubinoff, 1925. Photo courtesy of Mila Miller. *Middle Left:* Inscribed photo to Vasich from Albert Spalding, world-class violinist, 1927. Photo courtesy of Mila Miller. *Middle Right:* Srpski Seljaci, St. Steven's Cathedral, 1940. Front Row, George Rosich, Chris Samardzich, Roy Pizula, Tom Soso, Vaso Rosich and Milan Simich. Standing, Radovan Zvier, George Samardzich, Director Vaso Crljenica, Milo Pizula and Goyco Samardzich. Photo courtesy of Steve Crljenica. *Bottom Photos:* Dave Zupkovich Orchestra with Peter Vlajkovich, Joe Matacic and Tony Markulin, 1946. Photos courtesy of Mitzi Alexich.

*Top Left:* Banat Orchestra, 1912. Photo courtesy of Angie Trbovich. *Top Right:* Sveta Marich, Bogdan Todorovic and Miloj Ilich, 1950s. Photo courtesy of Miloj Ilich. *Middle Left:* The Balkan Strings, Bratso Tomich, Georgie Cavic and Zivan Katich, 1980. Photo courtesy of George Cavic. *Above Left:* Plavi Mjesec, Steubenville, 1948. Photo courtesy of Darleen Licina Tubbs. *Bottom Left:* Martha Kukich and her father Danny. Photo courtesy of Martha Kukich. *Above:* Hajduk Orchestra during performance with Aman, 1965. Photo by William Dorich.

*Top Left:* The Becari Orchestra, San Francisco, 1991. Back Row, Bill Davidovich, John Medan, Bob Medan, Ted Vukelich, Dusan Medan. *Middle Row,* Pavle Bunjevic, Paul Golubovich, Charity Vudin, Priscilla Palomino. Front Row, Elizabeth Claek, Sam Vudis, George Milinovich. Photo courtesy of Mitzi Alexich. *Middle Left:* Crljenica Brothers Continental Five. Seated, Steve and Paul. *Standing,* Bobby Warner, Vasil Crljenica and Mitch Dvorak. Photo courtesy of Steve Crljenica. *Top Right:* Del (Kachar) Casher with Less Paul. Photo courtesy of Del Casher. *Middle Right:* Del Casher as a young musician. Photo courtesy of Del Casher. *Left:* Trivanovich Sisters, 1990. Mickey, Angie, Honey and Vi. Photo courtesy of Honey Trivanovich Zimmerman. *Above:* President and Mrs. Ronald Reagan with Del Casher. Photo courtesy of Del Casher.

*Top Left:* Jorgovan Orchestra with Elijah Miskovic and Djoko Dokich on prim. Columbia Records, 1920. Photo courtesy of Mitzi Alexich. *Top Right:* The Rajsich Quintet, Youngstown, Ohio, 1930s. Sylvia, Nick, Jane, Joe and Stella Rajsich. Photo courtesy of Neda Susajic. *Middle Left:* Leona Wood performing her famous sword dance, UCLA Aman Ensemble, Greek Theater, 1964. Photo by William Dorich. Photo courtesy of The SNF *Above:* Album cover for Hajduk Orchestra, 1966. Photo by William Dorich. *Left:* Charles Kezman and *Right:* Ted Raddish of Hajduk Orchestra. Photos courtesy of Emma Raddish.

*Top Left:* Ljubavi Tamburitzans, 1964(?). Gertrude and Bess Kovacevich, R. Miljevich, Eli Miljevich, Rudy Verbos. Photo courtesy of Mitzi Alexich. *Top Right:* Zlatna Tambura, Aliquippa, PA, 1976. Photo courtesy of The Serb National Federation. *Middle:* Srpski Seljaci of St. Steven's Cathedral, 1956. In 1960 Peter Gaspich became the director of Srpski Seljaci. *Front Row,* Velma "Snookie" Milosevich, Romilda Lovrensky, Betty Kovacevich, Olga Milosevich, Director Lubo Kolakovich, Dorothy Samardzich, Violet Dakovich, Daisy Wimbish, Mary Dicklich. *Second Row,* Pete Jokola, Sarah Martinovich, Natalija Bokan, Ann Vance, Dolores Milicevich, Gloria Salata, Darlene Robles, Dorothy Milacich, Helen Popovich, Nuney Stoyanov. *Third Row,* Dorothy Kadan, Bob Samarzich, Zorka Prnjat, Mary Gibson, Olga Mitrovich, Vido Samarzich, Rosalie Savich, Doris Kolakovich, Donald Lubanko. *Fourth Row,* Marie Dragovich, Evelyn Rapaich, Natalie Durich, Steve Aleksich, Mike Radakovich, Micki Likich, Lex Ellesin, Mike Dicklich, Milan Putnick, Uros Bokan. Photo courtesy of Zorka Prnjat. *Above Left:* Dave Zupkovich Balkan Recorders, Youngstown, Ohio, 1959. Anthony Markulin, Pete Radakovich, Louis Markulin and Dave Zupkovich. Photo courtesy of Pete Radakovich. *Above Right:* The Rajsich Quintet today, Aliquippa, PA., Sylvia Relanovich, Nick Rajsich, Jane Mamula, Joe Rajsich and Stella Generalovich. Photo courtesy of Neda Susajic. *Bottom Right:* John Zevkovich Orchestra, John Zevkovich, Carl Schutzman, Carl Schutzman, Jr. and Bob Lalich, 1960s. Photo courtesy of The Serb National Federation.

*Top Left:* Vojan Popovich and Miloj Ilich, Los Angeles, 1950s. Photo courtesy of Miloj Ilich. *Top Right:* Vlajko Lugonja, Helen Tomich and Dave Zupkovich at an SSF Festival. Photo courtesy of The Serbian Singing Federation. *Middle Left:* Balkan Orchestra, with Matte Jurisich and Steve Crljenica, Chicago. Photo courtesy of Steve Crljenica. *Middle Right:* Star Serenaders, Richard Refkin, Steve Deanovich, Harry Zuvich and Jerry Banina, 1990. Photo courtesy of Ted Phillips. *Left:* Steve Barich. Photo courtesy of Mitci Alexich. *Above:* Srpski Seljaci Orchestra, 1956. Top Row, Smilka Radjenovich, Ted Raddish, Marie Dragovich, Olga Milosevich, Lawrence Merchep, Miki Likich. Seated, Zorka Prnjat, Velma Milosevich, Steve Crljenica, Petrena Johnson and Dorothy Harris. Photo courtesy of Zorka Prnjat. *Bottom Left:* Lubo Kolakovich who became the director of Srpski Seljaci at St. Steven's Cathedral with a fresh crop of musicians as marriage and children had their impact on the original orchestra. Photos courtesy of Zorka Prnjat.

*Top Left:* Sloga Orchestra, Farrell, PA, 1925. Photo courtesy of MIla Miller. *Top Right:* Isidor Bajic, 1962. Seated, Rada Stojic and Nikola Bakajin. Standing, Rudy Jovonov, Rudy Locnar and Louie Topalski. Photo courtesy of Nikola Bakajin. *Middle Row Left:* Dave Zupkovich Orchestra at Popovoch Brothers' Selo Club, Chicago, 1948. Photo courtesy of Mitzi Alexich. *Right:* Kosovo Orchestra, Pittsburgh. Milos Murkich, (unknown musician), Matt Perchak and Joe Lugares. Photo courtesy of Ted Philips. *Above:* Kosovo Orchestra, Milwaukee, final performance on May 25th, 1947, with Dorothy Ingich, Mitzi Sarenac, Mileva Pavich, Ann Obradovich and Mileva Borkovich. Photo courtesy of Mileva Borkovich Susnar. *Right:* Momchil Family Orchestra, Kansas City, 1921. *Bottom Right:* Pete Markovich. Photos courtesy of Helen Popovich.

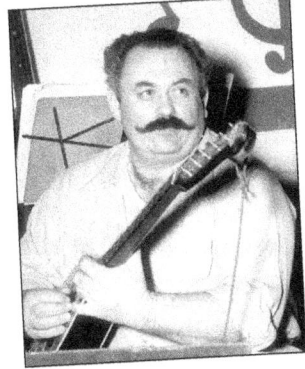

*Top Left:* Veseli Seljaci-California was organized in 1965 and is still an active orchestra in the San Francisco Bay Area. Front Row, George Pesut, Mike Vujovich, Al Bahr, Paul Sebesta and Mike Brkljacich. Standing, Caroline Bahr, Cele Benrath, Denise Quintell, Kathy Sulaver, Tanja Milajkovich, Joanne Wood, Betty Moomey, Marlene Sulaver, Nancy Bjeletich, Emily Sesich. Photo courtesy of Emma Raddish. *Top Right:* Nick Bezich Orchestra, 1921. Photo courtesy of Mitzi Alexich. *Middle Left:* St. Sava Jr. Tamburitzans, 1963. *Middle Right:* Canadian Prime Minister's wife, Mila Mulroney with the Balkan Serenaders, 1988, Niagara Falls. Photo courtesy of Frank Zajackowski. *Above:* St. Archangel Michael Jr,. Tamburitzans. *Right:* Lira Orchestra, Warren, Michigan. Ken Kosovec, Bogdan Topolski, Pero Pavlovich, Dennis Kosovec and Sanda Pavlovich. Photo courtesy of Ted Phillips. *Below:* Redwood Tams, Chicago. Photo courtesy of Mitzi Alexich.

*Top Left:* Orchestra Slavuj, Windsor/Detroit area, 1954. Bill Topolski, Mike Adams, Chic Skaljac and Sanda Pavlovich. Photo courtesy of Ted Phillips. *Top Middle:* Mita Bujotovich. Photo courtesy of the Serbian Singing Federation. *Top Right:* Rasha Radenkovich and Angelina Vlajkovich, king and queen of the ball. Photo courtesy of the Serbian Singing Federation. *Middle:* Milan Petrovich. Photo courtesy of the Serbian Singing Federation. *Above Left:* Mirko Roknich Orchestra, Canton, Ohio. Photo courtesy of Ted Phillips. *Above Right:* Edo Lubich. Photo courtesy of Nikki Lubich.

*Top:* Soko Orchestra with George Kahcar, 1928. Photo courtesy of Del Casher. *Second Row:* Pete Radakovich Orchestra, Canton, Ohio. Shown in photo is Pete Radakovich, his son Pete, Jr. on bass and Mike Rogich on brach. Photo courtesy of the Serb National Federation. *Right:* Novi Zivot Orchestra. Seated, Steve Stimac, George Laskarin, director Joe Nastav, Mihailo Kesely and Ann Nicksic. Standing, Helen Niksic, John Zafran, Rich Savage, Steve Deanovich and Rose Strcich. Photo courtesy of SSF. *Third Row:* Rich, Rob, George Ivancivich and Pete (?). Photo courtesy of The Serb National Federation. *Above Left:* Vatra Ziva, Columbus, Ohio. *Right:* Hajduk Orchestra on stage at UCLA, 1965. Michael Tomaiko, Milan Bosrock, Adele Raddish Chadwick, Charlie Kezman and Ted Raddish. Photo by William Dorich.

*Top Left:* Djoko Pribich Tamburitzans, began in 1934 in Massillon, Ohio, 1960. (L to R) George Matie, Fez Turkal, Etch Turkal, Johnny Nervo, Rudy Dolich, Jock Pribich and George Dorosky. Photo courtesy of Agnes Pribich. *Top Right:* Orchestra Starigrad, Dawn Radicevich, Jim Walker, Cyril Seso, Lisa Milena Simikic, Chuck Grosz and Mike Radicevich. Photo courtesy of Lisa Simikic. *Middle Left,* Dave Zupkovich Orchestra. Photo courtesy of Adam Popovich. *Middle Right:* Mladi Yugovichi Orchestra, Massillon, Ohio. Seated, Nick Turkal and Johnny Nervo. Standing, George Pribich, George Matie, Joe Bogovich, Mike Rogich, Tony Sepapak, 1941. Photo courtesy of Agnes Pribich. *Bottom:* The 1st Jr. Tamburitzians of St. Steven Cathedral. Directed by Lubo Kolakovich, 1959. Bottom Row, Dennis Jaich, Joan Cheyovich, George Spadier, Diane Spadier, Christine Jaich, Jovo Spadier, Nada Spadier and Max Dragovich. Middle Row, Dan Dakovich, Michelle Cheyovich, Michael Spadier, Nancy Popovich, Nick Kavic, Natalie Rafaelovich, Michael Dragovich, Barbara Krulic, and Steve Kavic. Back Row, John Milosevich, Mark Martinovich, Tomo Milosevich, Pete Zotovich, George Mrvichin and Donald Putnick. Photo courtesy of Helen Rafaelovich.

*Top:* S.S.S. Njegosh Choir, 1st Place winner of the Michael Pupin Cup, Akron, Ohio, 1940. *Above:* Sloboda Choir with Adam Popovich, dress rehearsal for the Eisenhower Presidential Inaguration. Photos courtesy of Mitzi Alexich.

### In Gratitude

*We wish to express appreciation to all of the participants who made this book possible. A special thank you to Mitzi Alexich, Del Casher, Steve Crljenica, Ted Phillips, Adam Popovich, Helen Popovich and Emma Raddish for providing many of the important photographs pertaining to tamburitza history. We also wish to acknowledge Paul S. Bielich, President of the Serbian Singing Federation and George Martich, President of the Serb National Federation for their cooperation in providing access to their archives.*

# Epilogue

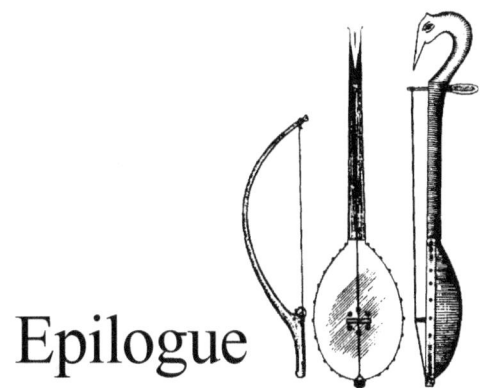

Frank Lloyd Wright once said, *"What good is all the art in a museum if the building lacks inspiration?"* By the same token, what good is the finest instrument in the world if the music played on it does not stir the soul?

For nearly 500 years the Serbian people lived under Ottoman oppression in which they were denied basic human rights—the right to an education, to own land, to worship freely and the right to use musical instruments as a form of artistic expression.

Prior to the Serbian defeat at Kosovo in 1389 and the eventual enslavement of the Serbian nation some 60 years later, Serbs had the enlightened accomplishments of the Adriatic Dynasty in the 12th century, the rich vitality of the Nemanjic Dynasty in the 13th century, over a hundred years of their own nationhood and the Serbian Orthodox Church which formed their identity.

Tsar Dusan's Code of Laws, studiously prepared during the years from 1349 to 1354, is recognized today by legal scholars to count among the leading law systems of the world. Serbs were not cooperative slaves, demonstrating that chains could not harness their spirit. The Jamaican people were also denied the use of musical instruments and resorted to reinventing their music on steel drums—just as the Serbs relied on the *gusle* and the songs of the *guslars* to orally maintain centuries of unwritten history. The unconquerable Serbian slaves also turned their adversity into creativity by inventing a *silent kolo* with the syncopated beat of their footsteps becoming the musical background of a dance that symbolized their very enslavement.

In the famous work, *The Death of a Guslar,* by Isidor Bajic (1875-1915), the poet reminds us that thousands of musicians were blinded by their oppressors, that the Ottoman Turks *"destroyed their worldly goods and harvested their hopes,"* but they could never make these blind *guslars* sing the praises of the pashas who murdered the sons and raped the daughters of the oppressed Serbian population.

This book is intended to reveal some of the rich musical and artistic accomplishments of the Serbian people—which they achieved in less than 200 years. Tamburitza music has become synonymous with the Serbian race, just as the melodic voices of the Serbian people have become their instruments against all forms of tyranny.

Helen Leah Reed's eloquent words ring with historic significance in 1998, as they did in 1916: *"The guslars, singing the heroic pesme, were hardly second in influence to the priests in fortifying the spirits of the suffering Serbs. The intense patriotism of the Serb was kept alive, indeed was often kindled, by the folk songs he had heard even in his cradle. Through all his troubles he has cherished the divine fire of nationality, even as the Vestals conserved the sacred flame."*

William Dorich

ABOUT THE PEOPLE WHO CREATED THIS BOOK

### WILLIAM DORICH—COMPILER • PRODUCER • DESIGNER

William Dorich's background includes more than 20 years in the printing industry prior to establishing his own publishing company, GM Books., in 1984. His firm has produced over 150 titles. Best known in the Serbian community for his articles that appeared in *The American Srbobran*, his views on the Civil War in Bosnia and Kosovo have been printed in the Washington Times, Heritage Southwest Jewish Press, The Wall Street Journal, The Chicago Tribune, International Herald Tribune and the Arizona Republic. For the 50th anniversary of the Serbian Holocaust, Mr. Dorich authored and compiled, *The Serbian Genocide—1941-45*. To commemorate the first visit of His Holiness Pavle, the Serbian Patriarch to the United States and to raise money for Serbian orphans, he designed, compiled and produced the 1992 book, *Kosovo*, for the Kosovo Charity Fund of the American Western Diocese. His newest book for the Diocese is *Hilandar's Octocentenary*, a commemoration of the 800th anniversary of the Serbian Monastery on Mount Athos. Mr. Dorich is a recipient of the *Order of St. Sava*, the highest award bestowed on a lay person by the Holy Synod of Serbian Bishops of the Orthodox Church.

### BASIL W. R. JENKINS—EDITOR

As a doctoral student, Mr. Jenkins studied with some of the outstanding Byzantinists of the 20th century. He is the author of The Greek Ethos, co-published by the UCLA Center for Medieval and Renaissance Studies and CAFAM, and his articles include "A Phase of the Monothelite Controversy: Attempts in the 7th Century A. D. for Ecclesiastical Union Between the Byzantine Imperial Church and the Armenian Church" and "Early Russian Gold, Silver, and Enamel work." The editor of 9 books, including the above mentioned book, Kosovo, and more than 100 articles, he has written and lectured extensively in the areas of history and art history. He was the director and curator of the Fowler Foundation Museum for 13 years and was later the curator for the Philosophical Research Society Art Collection.

### ANITA DORICH—RESEARCH • PROJECT DIRECTOR

Anita Dorich received her BSW from San Francisco State University and has had postgraduate training at U.C. Berkeley and U. S.C. She is trilingual, with fluency in Serbian and Spanish. She spent 20 years as a professional counselor at the Motion Picture & Television Fund in Hollywood. She has been president of Graphics Management since 1991 where she also manages research for all publications. She has been project director on more than 70 titles produced by GM Books, several for the Los Angeles Times and Simon & Schuster. She is currently in the process of authoring a work of her own.

www.ingramcontent.com/pod-product-compliance
Lightning Source LLC
Chambersburg PA
CBHW080553230426
43663CB00015B/2817